Don't Polish Your Ignorance

...It May Shine

DON'T POLISH YOUR IGNORANCE

...It May Shine

Sadhguru

Yogi, Mystic and Visionary

JAICO PUBLISHING HOUSE

Ahmedabad Bangalore Bhopal Bhubaneswar Chennai
Delhi Hyderabad Kolkata Lucknow Mumbai

Published by Jaico Publishing House
A-2 Jash Chambers, 7-A Sir Phirozshah Mehta Road
Fort, Mumbai - 400 001
jaicopub@jaicobooks.com
www.jaicobooks.com

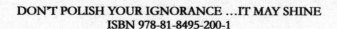

DON'T POLISH YOUR IGNORANCE ...IT MAY SHINE
ISBN 978-81-8495-200-1

First Jaico Impression: 2011
Twenty-seventh Jaico Impression: 2019

Printed by
Snehesh Printers, Mumbai

CONTENTS

For All Those Who Polish:
A PREFACE

❦

PART ONE   I

COMMUNION:
Satsangh, Fear, Faith, Joy, Presence

❦

PART TWO   63

CONNECTION:
Relationships, Suffering, Mind, Emotion

❦

PART THREE   145

COMPLETION:
Truth, Life, the Master

❦

For All Those Who Polish:

A PREFACE

There are only two types of people in the world, if we are to believe the author of this book: those who are seekers and know it, and those who are seekers and don't know it.

There is admittedly a third category: the mystics, the sages and the saints of this world. Presumably they have no need of such a book. But if you aren't a member of this tribe, this book could be for you.

Let's start with the second category. If you're a seeker who doesn't know it, you'll find several reasons to revisit this book. For one, this is a book that explores familiar areas of concern, gnawing human preoccupations. It talks of freedom, community, happiness, relationships, creativity, fear, anger, love, death — all that and more.

But perhaps your first discovery will be the author himself. Sadhguru is a mystic and a living master who embodies all the bewildering paradoxes associated with his ilk: the gentleness and the brutal directness, the abruptness and the compassion.

His voice is a distinct one: it is frank, bold, hard-hitting, funny and provocative. Above all, it is a voice that refuses to perpetuate the clichés of the archetypal Holy Man Discourse. Does he ask you to surrender? Does he urge you to believe? Does he advise you to vanquish desire? To choose good over evil? None of the above.

This is not your beaming, benign moralist who endorses virtue, harmony and universal brotherhood, seasoned with a comforting dose of guilt-assuaging New Ageism. This is not the voice of the scholar or the priest or the orator. It is instead a strange and yet compelling presence, one that speaks with an authority that could strike you as arrogant but never phony or sanctimonious, unfaltering but never unconsidered.

And that brings me to the first category. If you are a seeker and know it, the rewards of this book will be evident from the start. For when speaking of the existential journey, there are few who can match the depth and clarity, the subtlety, the precision, the fine-tuned discernment that Sadhguru brings to the subject. This is a man who knows the path — every roadblock, every diversion, every seductive neon billboard. And he's just as well acquainted with what it takes to be a seeker. If anything, he seems intimately familiar with it — that ancient ache, seemingly programmed into the human form, for more-ness and no-more-ness, for expansion and union, for completion and dissolution.

The persistent questions of seekers fill this book. It's all here — the pain, the confusion, the raging gut-level thirst, all that it means to be human and alive and wanting. And through it all are the clear, strong, unwavering tones of a master who reminds us that the only thing that lies between the human and the divine, the finite and the boundless, the seeking and the finding, is choice.

What does that choice entail? Not the acquisition of any path-breaking wisdom, but a determined refusal to strengthen one's ignorance, to reinforce one's deceptions, to 'gold-plate one's limitations'.

And if, at the end of this book, you find you're still in the dark, take heart. For Sadhguru never promises to allay your thirst, only to intensify it. He never promises to eradicate your darkness, only to deepen it. The danger, he tells us in no uncertain terms, does not lie in being in the dark — that can be dispelled for anyone who genuinely desires it — but in settling for an easy brilliance, a spurious radiance. The danger does not lie in seeking urgently, but in arriving cheaply.

"Don't polish your ignorance," he warns aphoristically, unforgettably, recurrently in the course of this book. "it may shine."

—Arundhathi Subramaniam

PART ONE

COMMUNION:

Satsangh, Fear, Faith, Joy, Presence

"A satsangh is not a spiritual club... your whole life should become a satsangh."

A satsangh is not a meeting place for people. It is not a club or an association. Generally, people meet in these kinds of forums for different purposes. There are drinking clubs, playing clubs, gambling clubs, even spiritual clubs – various types of associations where people meet for certain purposes. In that context, a satsangh is not a spiritual club. It is neither a place to socialize, to get to know people, nor is it a place to spend the evening.

'Sat' in Sanskrit means 'truth' and 'sangh' means 'to be in communion'. In other words, it is a way of being in touch with truth. It means to communicate with that reality which is beyond the reality you normally experience, to communicate with that dimension which is not in the day-to-day experience of life for most people. We should always be in satsangh but because our involvement with truth is part-time, at least one place should be dedicated entirely to it. (*Laughs*)

So what is needed to be in communion with truth? What we are referring to as truth is that which makes everything work in the existence. Regardless of all that you do, something is spinning the planet, something is making this heart beat and something is making the whole cosmos work. Childish minds always jump to conclusions as to what it is. We do not have to jump to any conclusions. But obviously something is making everything happen; that is very clear, isn't it? That is what we refer to as truth. To be in touch with truth, we do not have to go to the core of the galaxy, because the core of a human being is also the same thing.

For most people, the day-to-day experience of life is just a bundle of impressions gathered through perceptions. All the time you perceive something. You look at a tree, at the sky, at an animal, at a bird, at the people around you; all of these are certain transactions. All the time these transactions are happening through your five senses, either by seeing, hearing, smelling, tasting, or touching. All the time in so many ways you are absorbing impressions of millions of forms of life and other objects around you.

What you normally call 'life' is just the constant happening of this transaction. How you transact or communicate with a certain aspect of life fundamentally depends on how you have done it before. What kind of impressions you gather of somebody who is sitting in front of you right now is simply decided by the past impressions you have within you. In other words, in this way of perceiving life, there is no sense of freedom. This kind of perception is just a reinforcement of bondage, because you experience things only the way your mind is conditioned to experience them all the time.

When we say 'satsangh', we are looking at being free from these impressions and this kind of perception. What perception means is this: right now if you look at me, it is just a certain energy transaction. Actually, what you call life is just a movement of energy. Energy is always dynamic, constantly in motion in so many ways. So this is a constant energy transaction. It goes on all the time between subject and object.

Because this whole transaction happens between object and subject, you need two entities. But if there are two entities, there is no spirituality. If you and the other exist, if God and devil exist, if heaven and hell exist, then there is no spirituality. Whether you communicate with a stone or you communicate with God, it is the same. It is the same level of ignorance, because there are still two entities. Duality still exists.

This splitting of the world between you and the other has happened to you out of your identification with the little things which you are not. This division of the world, this division of creation has happened to you only because you have identified yourself with this little piece of flesh. You have made the division, which is a falsehood.

So, when we say 'satsangh', we want to communicate with that which is true. A satsangh is that dimension where you are not trying to perceive something; you want to perceive yourself. Now you may say, "Oh, yes, I do perceive myself."

This is a deception, because what you have perceived is not you. The perceiver is still there, saying, "I know myself." This is a lie because the knower and the known are still separate.

The way you look at me right now, you cannot look at yourself because the one who sees and that which is seen are still separate. It is just that you are playing the game of withdrawing into deeper and deeper boundaries. It is the same game that you are playing on different levels.

Those people who are struggling with things and with others around them and those people who are struggling with gods and heavens are not in any way different. They are both glorifying their ignorance because the perceiver and the perceived are still separate. The known and the knower are still separate. In other words, it is the same ignorance being polished.

A satsangh is not meant to be a situation to glorify your ignorance, or to move from one level of ignorance to another. It is to perceive that which cannot be perceived.

How can one perceive that which cannot be perceived? You may think, "I perceive that which cannot be perceived." This again, is a trick. If you can simply be here, ignoring everything that you can perceive, you will see something else becomes alive. That something else can be referred to by any name, but here we just refer to it as truth.

It is not necessary that only a particular meeting be seen as a satsangh; your whole life should become a satsangh. Since your whole life happens either on the level of thinking or emoting, this is the only way you know life. The whole process of growing with a guru means being with that which cannot be perceived. You ignore everything that can be perceived so that the subjectivity of who you are suddenly becomes present.

The very process of satsangh means that you go into a state where you do not exist. You cease to exist as a person. You stop identifying with yourself so that the subjectivity becomes everything. There is nothing to perceive. You simply sit there. This is the very basis of everything that you can call spiritual.

In order to be this way you need to be in a certain presence. Without an overpowering presence, you cannot drop your own identifications because it is all that you have. You will naturally cling to those things you identify yourself with, starting with your body, your ideas, your likes, your dislikes, your relationships. Without that you cannot sit here as a human being.

If you just sit here and completely strip yourself of everything that you identify yourself with — and if you manage to throw everything down — then you will see there is no such thing as 'me', but there is a huge presence. There is a tremendous, overwhelming presence. Unless a person experiences this presence he has not taken any spiritual steps in his life yet. Maybe he is thinking of spirituality — simply thinking and hesitating all the time.

Now you will say, "You told us spirituality means ultimate

freedom, liberation, but now you are talking about destroying us." (*Laughs*) This is always the struggle in a human being: he thinks freedom means getting somewhere. Wherever you go, you will not be free; please see that. Wherever you may go in your life, you will not know freedom.

I do not usually talk about this, but generally, there has been so much talk about surrender everywhere. The moment thinking, logical, educated minds hear the word surrender, they build forts around themselves. It is dangerous for them because they are free-thinking people who are trapped in the mess of their own minds. To them surrender is for slaves, for the ones who are defeated.

When we use the word, 'surrender', it means that you surrender that which is false and everything that you are is just a falsehood. What you call 'myself' is just an identification that you have taken on in your life. Otherwise, what have you got to surrender? You really have nothing. When you realize this, you have surrendered. When you surrender the wall that you have built, everything becomes one.

Only when you merge with the existence are you free. As long as you and this existence are separate, there is no such thing as freedom. There cannot be any freedom, you understand? True freedom can happen only when you are not. As long as you are still there, where is the question of freedom? It is just that you may enlarge your prison walls, but bondage is still there. As long as you exist, there is bondage. When you surrender this illusory wall that you have built, this illusory wall of separation between you and existence, then everything is one.

Satsangh, in its ultimate sense, means that you surrender the wall that you have built. This wall does not exist, but you believe it exists. All that you are surrendering is your illusion, not reality. Reality is not something that you can create. Reality is that which contains you. It holds you. It is in the lap of reality that you exist. If you surrender the illusion, reality happens. It is not that it happens: it already is, but it happens to you. It comes into your experience.

Right now, in your experience you have become a whole world by yourself. What you call 'myself' is just a bundle of impressions, a whole garbage bin of impressions that you have gathered from everywhere around you. With all these multiple impressions you have built a world of your own, and this world is not the reality. Every moment, even to exist here physically, you have to communicate with the rest of existence. Even your breath is a communication on the physical level. If you break your communication with existence even for one moment, this being cannot exist. But you go about believing that you exist separately by yourself, and that you have got nothing to do with anything else. But every moment, even in the physical reality that you are in touch with, you cannot exist without this communication.

It is not that satsangh has to happen in a particular room or a hall. For those who are willing, it is happening all the time. In a room or a hall, we are trying to create an atmosphere where it would become easier for a person. As I mentioned earlier, without a certain presence, which seems to be much larger than yourself, dropping your identifications becomes difficult because it is like jumping into a void. Once you feel something, which is bigger than yourself, it becomes a little easier to keep yourself — or what you think of as yourself — aside. That is what satsangh is.

"Oh, this is too much, how do I become like this? We just came to meet you. All this is too much!" (*Laughter*) You have to come to a satsangh with a different attitude than the way you go to some associations, meetings, clubs and anywhere else. You go to all those places to manifest your exclusiveness. Satsangh is to drop your exclusiveness.

As I said before, satsangh means a communion with truth. You do not know what truth is: people have been talking about truth, the scriptures have been screaming about it, but you do not know what it is. So how can you commune with it?

Right now, when you sit with a guru, he is the nearest thing to truth that you know. That also you are not sure of. As far as you are concerned, you are not sure whether he is in truth or not. All you can see is that he seems to be at least in a little higher level of existence than you are. That is all you can see. He may or may not be in truth, but you have no way of knowing. The only thing that you can recognize is that he seems to be much clearer than you are about everything. He seems to be more in control of everything than you are. He seems to be at least one step higher than whatever you think you are.

The reason why you are sitting with a guru is that you see that he is sitting in a little more elevated place than you are. Whether he is sitting on the top of the world, or the end of the world, or beyond the world, you do not know. But definitely he is sitting in a more elevated place than you are. Even if you do not know whether you will get to the end of the world or beyond the world, at least you want to get where he is, to the next peak.

So when you sit in a satsangh, you sit totally with me. Do not worry about what is happening to somebody, be absolutely with me. Whatever somebody does, that is not your business. Your business is just to be with me.

─────◦❧◦─────

"You cannot become willing. Only when you have no will of your own, you are truly willing."

Questioner: You have said that in order to realize the ultimate one has to become willing. How can I become willing?

Sadhguru: You cannot become willing. Only when you have no will of your own you are truly willing. When you have a will of your own you stand up like a stone. It is just that this world, the people around you, and your education etc have always tried to teach you how to conquer. You can conquer stones. You can conquer patches of land. Maybe you can conquer physical bodies, but you cannot ever conquer even a single person.

Now, if knowing the ultimate is what you want, then the only way is to surrender, not to conquer. But for the logical mind surrender is disgraceful. Surrender is one thing that you do not want to do, because in surrendering you will come to an end.

This whole need to conquer comes from the fear of losing yourself. The very need to conquer something or somebody has come to you because there is a deep fear of losing yourself on many levels. Because you do not know how to handle that fear, you want to conquer people. You want to conquer more and more things. You want to acquire more and more — wealth, people, power, relationships etc — because otherwise you feel inadequate. You feel so inadequate that you feel that the very way you are created is not enough. Without all the things that you have gathered around yourself, you feel that you are not enough, that you are insufficient.

At the same time, you also say you believe in God. If he is the creator, and if he has created such a lousy being who feels insufficient all the time, there is something wrong with him. Is it not? (*Laughs*) If God created you — and you even say that he created you in his own image — and if his image is such a poor one that constantly feels insufficient and inadequate in life, then I would say "Poor God!" It is not you who needs to be saved. It is he who needs to be saved! (*Laughs*)

This inadequacy has come not because you are made that way. It has come because you have identified yourself with little things, and when you look at the vastness of the existence, you feel so small and lost. When your whole identification fundamentally is rooted in this little bit of flesh that walks about on this planet, then naturally you feel very, very inadequate. So, you have to prove yourself every moment of your life. People around you have to praise you and tell you that you are special, and constantly boost you all the time. Otherwise you feel lost.

Now to become willing means not identifying yourself with the limited. That is all it means. Now the question is, "How do I do that? This limited self is all I know…"

It is to handle this issue that people created a device and they started talking to you about God. They said, "Drop the identification with little things, and identify with God — something that you cannot see, something that is everything." But the problem with this approach is that now you have reduced what you call God also to another physical form like yourself, and you are identified with that form. On top of that, my god and your god are quarrelling. They keep waging wars against each other, which is of no use.

Every device that is created needs to be overhauled periodically, because it gets corrupted over a period of time. Once people realize the mechanics of the device, the device will not function for them anymore. New devices have to be constantly created because the device itself is of no importance. How well it works is all that matters. Now you got stuck with the limited idea of God also. This is just like me pointing a finger and saying "Look at the flower," but you get stuck with my finger and miss the flower completely.

So, these devices for shifting your identification from one thing to another are tricky and dangerous sometimes. It may take you a whole lifetime to release yourself from the next level of identity unless there is a live guru around you who constantly keeps breaking you. If by some good fortune, you do not run away — because you only like people who boost you, not somebody who breaks you (*Laughs*) — and you allow yourself to be broken in different steps, the process can be hastened.

But the whole game is such that he has to do the job with you very diplomatically. He cannot directly break you. If he has to go around you and create a whole situation before he knocks you once on your head, then it would take a long time. (*Laughs*) So, he is patient because he is not in a hurry, but you had better be in a hurry!

That is why I say, do not try to become willing. Just stop identifying yourself with what you consider to be yourself. But right now you cannot simply be, because your mind goes on identifying itself with anything and everything. If you have to identify with something, do not identify yourself with that which boosts you, identify yourself with that which breaks you.

"How aware you are is how alive you are. From life to death this is all the difference."

Questioner: I wanted to know what is going on during the Dance of Destruction[1] in the Samyama Program[2], when everyone is going crazy? What has this altered state of consciousness got to do with the experience of truth?

Sadhguru: When we say Dance of Destruction, we need to understand what it is that we are trying to destroy.

I am talking about this process of destruction in a very positive sense, not a negative sense. As you may know, in India, god is seen as the destroyer. He is seen as a destroyer because the idea is that if god does not destroy you, he is not a good god, because all your problems, your suffering, and your struggles in this world have come only because you have constructed yourself as a person, unconsciously. You are an unconscious construction.

Unknowingly, you did something and got stuck with it; you are unable to destroy it. Now, the one who is supposed to be above you, if he does not destroy this, if he does not help you to destroy this, he is no good, isn't it? So in Indian culture, the divine was never seen as a savior. He is not there

[1] A meditative process that is a part of the Samyama Program conducted by Sadhguru.

[2] A highly advanced meditation program conducted by Sadhguru where participants, who undergo extensive preparation for forty days prior to the program, experience deep meditative states.

to save you; he is there to destroy you.

So, the ancient prayers were not, "O God, save me," or "O God, give me this or give me that." The prayer was just "O God, destroy me! Please destroy me the way I am so that I can become one with you. Please destroy me the way I am, so that I do not have to exist in separation from you, because the basis of my whole struggle is just that I am separate from you. Please destroy this."

Similarly, everything that I have devised for people is just a process of destruction: destroying the limited so that they can become unlimited. You can feel the unbounded only if you become unlimited. There is no other way. You can become unbounded only if you are willing to destroy the limited.

Now, you have been through various processes from the first day of Isha Yoga Program[1] to whatever you are calling as the Dance of Destruction. In the Samyama Program, every device has been carefully structured so that it destroys you. If you give yourself completely, you will see in the very first day of Isha Yoga Program, when I talk about rules, I am trying to destroy your limited nature. When I say 'rules', I am not just talking about the rules of civility, or the rules of the street, or traffic rules. I am talking about all the rules in this existence. If you start experiencing all the rules in this existence as your rules, then who are you? You must be unbounded. There is no other way to feel.

---

[1] A generic name given to the scientifically structured spiritual programs designed by Sadhguru and offered by Isha centers around the world.

So, it is a device to destroy you. You did not put it deep enough into yourself. You just used it to some extent and you found little benefits. You just went home and said, "Okay, the rules of the home are my rules." A little bit of you was destroyed in this process, so suddenly you had a better relationship with the people around you. Life around you became a little smoother and you thought, "That's great. That is enough. Yoga is working for me." (*Laughs*)

These are the kinds of petty benefits that people are always seeking, and within a few weeks of life running smoothly, they get either bored with it, or sick of it. Then they start believing that the only way to be is to break the rules. After some time, they suddenly find that, "Yes, by just following these rules relationships are smoother, but what is the point? Let me break some rules." (*Laughs*) The itch comes, doesn't it?

So when I am talking about making the rules yours, I am not talking about just making your family situation happen smoothly. I am talking about destruction, absolute dissolution into them. Every single device is like that.

Because you did not budge from all these subtle devices, we put you through an intense process, where either you have to be destroyed, or your body has to be destroyed. (*Laughs*) We put you into such intense processes where you were really destroyed at least for a few moments. When you found that you were destroyed, when you found what you consider as yourself has gone, you found there is a huge presence. You can call this presence myself if you want, or you can call it Shiva, if you want, or you can call it God, if you want. You can call it whatever you want, but there is a massive presence, so overwhelming.

So this destruction is not about destroying something outside of yourself, though you almost broke the meditation hall in the process. (*Laughs*) It is about destroying that which you have built within yourself: that which does not exist but which you believe exists. It is the destruction of illusion.

If you are really aware, we do not have to make you jump around to do that. You can just sit here and do it. But right now your awareness is only to the extent that is sufficient for your survival. Only to that extent you are aware. Now when you are driving your car on the street, you are aware enough not to drive into the tree. You know that you have to keep it on the street. This awareness has come from the basic survival instinct. You have not done anything to become more aware beyond the need to survive.

If you move into a higher intensity of awareness, then these things would come naturally to you. If you become really aware, then everything that is not true will fall off. Only that which is true will be. Then we do not have to make you jump and do this and that.

You know there are many masters who use very violent methods, really violent ones, with their disciples who do not budge with subtle methods. These disciples just go on playing tricks, misinterpreting the subtleness of the method all the time. So the only way was to take a club and hit them on the head, or whatever else. Really violent methods were used. Not because the master enjoys causing injury or pain to somebody. It is just because unless there is pain, most people never look at themselves. They always look far away.

Please see this: when you are walking and looking around, you are not really aware of yourself. But let us say, suddenly a thorn pierces your body, now all attention is on that spot, is it not? At least a little part of your body becomes fully aware when something pokes you. Otherwise, you are like a TV monitor, like a security camera. You are all the time grasping everything, and yet not grasping anything. (*Laughs*)

So, the 'Dance of Destruction' is just shaking you up to a certain intensity of awareness. The word 'awareness' has always been so badly misunderstood and misinterpreted. When I say awareness, I do not mean anything other than aliveness. Awareness is aliveness. How aware you are is how alive you are. The difference between life and death is just that.

For example, when I call out your name, if you become aware of that, I see that you are awake. But when I call out your name if you are not aware of it, then I think maybe you are asleep. Let us say I come and shake you, and then if you become aware, I know you are alive but were asleep. Now even when I come and shake you up, if you are not aware of it, then I assume you are dead.

So moving on the journey from life to death is just moving from awareness to unawareness. What you call 'life' or what you call 'aliveness' is a certain level of awareness. So the question is how alive do you want to become? If you have any sense you would want to become absolutely alive, is it not?

The reason why you lower your levels of aliveness is because in death there is safety and tremendous security. Though people are afraid of death, they are always seeking it, courting it in many ways, because death is such a relief. They do not have the courage to simply step into it, but they are courting it all the time. They want it, because that saves them from all the turmoil and struggle of life.

In so many ways you are trying to reduce the intensity of your life, of your aliveness. Reducing aliveness means infusing death. You are bringing it into your life in stages because you do not have the courage to just jump into it.

So, the spiritual process means cranking up the aliveness to such a peak that both life and death disappear from you. Then there is no distinction between the two for you. That is what was being done to you.

"An ashram is not your home. An ashram is only for those people who have chosen to be homeless."

Questioner: When you have a sincere desire to know God or experience God, it seems like the easiest thing to do is to go to an ashram or a forest and be alone. But you have said that is not always appropriate.

Sadhguru: I never said going to an ashram is inappropriate. I only said maybe it is not necessary for you. Why I say so is that people have a need for a home. Home means something that they own, or that they possess. They need something which gives them security, or something they can lean upon. It may be a one-bedroom apartment, or it may be a million-dollar set up; it does not matter what it is, but you need something that you can consider yours, is it not?

So when you have this need, if you move into an ashram, all that you will seek is a larger home. Because your little family has failed you, you seek a larger family. This may make you comfortable; it may fulfill one aspect of your life, but this is not spiritual. You would be wasting the spiritual dimension of living in a certain space like an ashram — a sacred space.

Why I call an ashram a sacred space is because it is created as a device where things that would take a lot of time to happen elsewhere, can happen very fast. One thing is this: so far you have lived with only two or four people in your family. But you are unable to bear these people's expectations, their emotions, their nonsense. Now, if I put you in a place where there are two hundred people — along with their expectations, their emotions, their tearing at you — I think it will mature you very quickly. (*Laughs*)

But if you are looking for an escape, an ashram is not the place to go to. If you see it as a possibility, then yes, it is a beautiful place to go to. One should not be seeking a more secure home in an ashram. An ashram is not your home. An ashram is only for those people who have chosen to be homeless; intentionally they want to be homeless. They have chosen to be orphans and be by themselves. They have everything, but still they chose to be like absolute orphans. They have no need to lean upon anybody.

This is being done so that your energies get centered in a certain way. All the support that you have for your emotions, your thoughts, your likes and dislikes are just being pulled away. In an ashram you do not decide what you are going to eat for today's dinner. That itself shatters you. It is unbearable, is it not? (*Laughs*) There is so much variety in your life that making a decision has become a problem. Just a simple thing like what to eat today or what to wear today, if it is not their decision anymore, it can be shattering for people.

So if you are looking at an ashram as a possibility for transformation or if you are looking at it as a possibility to live in as an absolutely homeless person by choice, and not because you are destitute, then an ashram is a good place to go to. But if you are looking for an alternative home, then an ashram is not a good place to go to; you should not go there.

—◦❦◦—

"I never asked you to trust me. I never use that word with people because it has been badly corrupted."

Questioner: You say that in order to expand, we must experiment with life and see for ourselves, but we are not to believe anything. But then it seems that in order to grow spiritually, a tremendous trust and faith in the guru is needed. So what is the difference between the two?

Sadhguru: See, belief springs from your expectations. When you say "I believe in you," what you are saying is, "You must live according to my expectations." You have a set of rights and wrongs, goods and bads, the divines and devils within you, and you are expecting me to live according to them. That is what you mean by saying "I believe in you."

Suppose I do something, which does not fit into the field of your rights and wrongs. Then the first thing that you are going to do is come to me and say, "See, I believed in you, but you did this." So all you are trying to do is an attempt to mold me into your limitations.

If your guru can be contained within your limitations, then you had better not go anywhere near him because he will be of no help to you. He may solace you, he may comfort you, but such a man brings bondage; he will not bring liberation to you.

Now when you say 'having trust', that is different. Trust is your quality. It is not subject to anything else. It is simply there. When you say, "I trust you," what it means is that you are not subjecting me to any particular kind of action, or to any set of expectations that you have within you. When you say, "I trust," it means that "It does not matter what you do, I trust you." That is not falling into the framework of your limitations. Belief is within the framework of your limitations; trust is not in the framework.

By the way, I never asked you to trust me. I never use that word with people because it has been badly corrupted. The reason why anyone speaks about trust is to raise you beyond your own likes and dislikes, beyond your own 'goods' and 'bads', and beyond your own limitations, and your whole personality.

Now, the basis of your whole personality is your likes and dislikes. What you like, what you do not like is what has built this person. When you say, "I trust you," the very feeling of trust raises you beyond this bundle of likes and dislikes. It means "No matter what you do, I trust you." It does not mean, "If you do this I trust you, but if you do not do that I do not trust you."

So, if you really want to make use of somebody's presence you must be willing to allow that presence to overwhelm you, overpower you, and destroy you in such a way that when you are with him, you are no more yourself. At least for those few moments in his presence, you are not yourself. In other words, who you consider yourself to be is absent in his presence. If this does not happen, whatever else you are talking about is of no significance.

So when people speak about trust, this is what they mean: that you allow someone else to enter you. If you have to allow someone else to enter you, you have to become vulnerable. It is dangerous, you know? Once he enters you, you do not know what he will do, and you could be subject to anything, isn't it? That is always the fear involved with trust.

The very reason why you have built walls around yourself is that when you made yourself vulnerable, somebody did something, which did not fit into the framework of your expectations. This became a big fear, and you built walls around yourself. Then you thought, "Oh, we should not allow anybody beyond this wall because if they come inside, they may do this or that." Now when you say, "I trust you," what you are saying is that you are willing to pull that wall down.

Pulling that wall down does not mean that somebody else has to live within the framework of your expectations. It means that whatever that person may do, it is okay with you. So what I am telling you is that it is the presence of the guru – the quality of who he is – that does things to you, in terms of bringing down your walls. The moment you create this situation that you are not bothered about what is going to happen to you, that itself is transformation.

Whenever things happened around Jesus, when his followers said, "Oh, you performed this healing," he always said, "It is not me. It is you." He was probably not even aware of their suffering, but since they opened up, something happened. Opening up became easy in his presence. That is all. And here I am. (*Laughs*)

The time-frame that I have with people is limited. So I am just making myself available only as a presence, not as a person. As a person I am just keeping a certain face, in many ways, within the framework of your expectations. If I have to use my person also as a device, then it needs much more trust and much more time.

People who are with me in larger time-frames find me to be an impossible person. I am not being like that with you. (*Laughs*) I am not yet using my person as a device because it needs a larger time-frame; otherwise you will run away. You will definitely run away if I start using my person as a device. Only with a few people I use my person as a device; with others I only use my presence. You understand what I am saying?

Questioner: I do not. What is the difference?

Sadhguru: See, right now you are a certain person. As we have already looked at this at different times, this personality is an unconscious happening or an unconscious creation of yours. This personality that you call 'myself' is in some ways an accident, depending upon what kind of situations you have been exposed to. That is how you took the impressions into you and you became this kind of person. And this person that you call 'myself' is still evolving. So, your person or your personality is constantly evolving by being beaten around by life. Whichever way life beats you, you will become that kind of shape and form.

The situations around you are not expert sculptors, but they will make you in the end. If you are being beaten around by every event that happens around you, in the end you will be a very ugly shapeless person – that is for sure – because it is an unconscious creation.

By reacting to everything that happens around him, slowly this person finds shape. Let us say the family was good to him and people around were loving to him, so, as a result, this person has a certain reasonable shape. Suddenly somebody clashes with him and this person gets all twisted-up. Now he's got ugly sharp edges to him, which were not there earlier. So, your personality is constantly being constructed by external situations: the way they beat you around, the way they kick you around, that is what your person is.

So, who is that person whom you call a guru? He is not a person. The whole process of realization means that he has transcended the person and then carefully crafted his personality as it is necessary for the kind of role he wants to play in the world.

You are also doing this in certain limited ways. Let us say you have become a country music star. Now you are not going to wear a turban. You are going to wear a ten gallon hat. You are building your personality to suit your activity, yes?

In a limited way you are doing this on the surface. A being who has experienced himself, or who is experiencing himself beyond those limitations, does it in a very deep way. Every aspect of his life he structures as it is necessary for the role that he has chosen to play. It is a conscious construction. Now when it is a conscious construction, it is just a device and it is not a bondage anymore. Any moment he can just pull it down.

Actually, before we started talking about creating the Dhyanalinga[1], we first spoke about it in a certain program called the 'Wholeness Program', which was a ninety day program with a certain group of people. I gathered these people in one place in a committed way for ninety days, in the middle of a forest, and then I started changing my person. Every day they started seeing a new person. Some of them were terrified, some of them were overjoyed, some of them were broken, and some of them went mad. But they started seeing that every day I was building a new kind of person, because I was stepping into a new role. The earlier person could not have suddenly fulfilled that purpose.

Because your ability to experience my presence is very limited, you mostly experience my person. Generally your mind judges, "Oh, he's a good man", "He's a bad man" – this is how you can experience a person. "Oh, he is a polite

---

[1] A powerful energy form with intense vibrational energies, this is the first of its kind to be completed in over 2,000 years. Consecrated by Sadhguru in June 1999, the Dhyanalinga multi-relgious yogic shrine at the Isha Yoga Centre in Coimbatore offers a unique space that induces deep states of meditativeness in all who sit in its presence. It subscribes to no particular faith or belief system, and requires no ritual, prayer or worship.

man"; "He is a generous man"; "He is an impolite man"; "He is an abrasive person." This is how you experience my presence, isn't it? So, your ability to experience the presence is just in very rare moments. Most of the time you are just clinging to the person.

So, the kind of personality I had developed till the moment I announced the Dhyanalinga, I changed it completely at that program. A few people left. A few people, who were deeply involved with the work, left because they said, "This is not fair. This is not the man that we came with."

I had prepared the situation. I had told them it is going to happen, but they did not take it like it was really going to happen. When it really started happening, suddenly the man that they knew, they loved and trusted, suddenly that person started to disappear and a totally new person came up. They said, "Oh, we do not want this man", and so they left. I warned them, "Many of you will leave as I evolve. This many of you will leave." They didn't believe it and said, "No, no, we are committed. We like what you are doing. We are with you." (*Laughs*) But when I started structuring a different person, because I had to fulfill a completely different role, it became too shattering for them.

This is happening to you in your lives. The people whom you think you love and trust, when their personality begins to change even in the smallest ways, your reactions become violent, is it not?

So a realized person constructs his personality fully consciously, the way it is necessary for his work. And even now the way I operate as a person in different places is very different. It may be shocking to you if you see me in other kinds of situations. Suddenly you feel, "I do not know this man. Who is he?" Now, because you have fallen into the comfort of knowing this kind of person, when you see another kind of person you are unable to deal with it.

So, generally I carefully craft a personality — a personality that people do not know whether to love or to hate. One moment you think, "I am really in love with this man." Next moment you are like, "I really hate this man." Both of these emotions are not allowed to cross certain lines. Within that you are constantly being thrashed around so that after some time you know this is not a person. This is not a human being. Either he is a beast or he must be the divine. (*Laughs*)

"Faith means that who you are right now is not important for you. It means something else has become far more important than yourself."

Questioner: How do we deal with those moments when fears really hit us in the face in this spiritual process? We may unconsciously run away, or want to run away from them. How do we deal with those moments?

Sadhguru: The first thing is for you to recognize that right now you exist within certain limitations. Why right from the Introductory Talk, I am trying to destroy all your belief systems is because these belief systems are so deceptive. You really believe that you trust God. But let us say your neighbor's dog chases you. Then you forget all about God and you run in terror, isn't it?

These belief systems give you a great sense of security, which is a great deception. So, the first thing is to recognize that right now you exist as a limited human being, with fears and anxieties. In fact, fear is the most basic and fundamental emotion within you.

Almost every other emotion springs from that. You do not know love. You only know fear. The fear adjustment between two people is called love. How we handle our fears between the two of us, is what you refer to as a love affair.

Clearly, fear exists in you. Whether it is a spiritual process, or your career, or driving on the street, or simply taking a walk, there is fear. Maybe most of the time you are not aware of it and it takes certain extreme situations for you to realize that there is fear in you.

Let us say, you have been driving happily every day, nonchalantly, and suddenly today somebody came and crashed into you, or you went and crashed into something. Only a little bit of injury and pain happened, but tomorrow you will sit in the car, and pray to God – you have to call God to drive. All those days you were just swinging around on the street, but now suddenly you need God's assistance to drive. It is not that there was no fear in you to begin with. There was fear in you. It just took a certain painful situation to make you aware of it.

You are in fear in many ways. If you ask me, you are fear itself. It is just that by making certain arrangements in life you try to keep fear beneath the surface. When your arrangements do not work, it pops up, isn't it?

So, fear is also naturally there in every aspect on the spiritual path. It is very natural. If you are aware of the fear, then it is good. It is good that you are aware that you have fear before taking the next step and still you do not succumb to that fear.

Now to overcome this, and to continue walking the path, there is one most essential thing you must have, and that is commitment. To be committed is the only thing you can do. You are incapable of faith. You are really incapable of faith. Please look at this. Your faith is like this: if something other than what you like happens, it will evaporate.

But you are capable of commitment. So in the Isha Yoga Program, we start with a seven-day commitment. No matter what happens in these seven days, you will still sit there — whether you like it or not, whether you are thrashed or robbed. In these seven days, you stay there.

So, now if these seven days of being committed has worked for you, you extend this: "Okay, for the next three years I will be committed. No matter what happens, whether I like it or not, whether I get problems or benefits from this spiritual process, for three years I'm committed to pursue this." If three years have been good, and if it really has brought growth into you, then make it thirty years: "For thirty years I'm committed, no matter what happens in the process. Even if I am taken to hell it is okay because I am committed."

This is the only way you can rise beyond your limitations and fears. Otherwise every step when fear comes, you will ask yourself, "Should I really do this? No, do I really need this?" And if people around you support this all the time, you will not get anywhere.

If you talk about faith without being in faith, it will be just a waste of life. With this commitment, slowly faith may happen to you. Faith is not something that you can force upon yourself. Faith is not something that you can do to yourself. Faith means you are not. Only then there is faith. Faith means who you are right now is not important for you. Something else has become far more important than you.

This can happen to you. As you go into higher levels of experiences within yourself, a time will come when you say, "If you lead me into hell, it is okay. If you are the devil himself, it is all right with me." When you become like this, then you will see everything that needs to happen will happen by itself. It is not that I have to do something to you. It will just happen because once you drop the wall, the existence will happen, reality will happen.

So, my business, my job is not to bring reality to you. My business is just to create a situation where you are willing to drop your wall. The rest will happen by itself. That is not something that I do.

See, right from the basic process of teaching the Isha Yoga

practices, they were not just taught to you as practices. We did not call you to some health club and teach you how to breathe, how to hold your breath, how to bend your body, or how to stand on your head. We taught you each practice while creating a whole atmosphere around it. Before we taught you the practice, we put other inputs into you, which brought a certain sense of opening in you. That is how the device is structured so that you become committed to it.

The practice is also an important part of it, but your commitment is to the path. During those seven days, maybe you only intellectually grasped what Isha Yoga is, but your commitment is to make it an absolute reality in your life in the next seven days. Let this commitment be your goal in the next seven days, the next seven moments, or the next seven years, or the next seven lifetimes — that you are in absolute acceptance.

Becoming absolute acceptance simply means pulling down all the walls that you have created. Every device that was employed in those seven days was just a different way of approaching the same walls, and knowing how to pull them down. So being committed to the practice is also just that.

What you are doing as yogic practices is just to give you an experience of being a little beyond this physical frame in order to pull down the physical wall, because that is the most difficult wall, and that is the most basic wall. That is the foundation of all the other walls.

The foundation of all the other barriers that you have created in your life is the body. Only because you have a body, 'me' has become a separate entity. This piece of flesh is the foundation of all the other walls that you have built. So with the yoga practice you are digging up the foundation. Without doing anything, if you simply go on digging the foundation, one day the wall can collapse. It is possible. But if while you are digging the foundation, you also start knocking down the other stones on the top, the possibility of the wall collapsing becomes faster.

So your commitment is that you are pulling down the walls consciously all the time. Every device that was in the program is just this, please see. It is just different presentations so that at least one of them you use fully and it will happen. You do not have to get the whole seven days of the program. If you get any one day of it, that will be a complete path by itself. Nothing else is necessary for you.

"Your survival happens only with receptivity, but in your need to survive you are just destroying the very basis of your survival."

Questioner: I have been trying to look at my life as a game. Even though I set out to look at the different roles in my life as a game, I end up forgetting that I am playing. Because I am very competitive, I get caught up in the playing. Why is this happening? It is either a part of a certain natural process or it's because I am a fool.

Sadhguru: I know that you are a fool. If you also know it, it is good. Just my knowing it is no good. (Laughs)

Questioner: I know. I know deeply. I just do not know how to get out of it.

Sadhguru: Now that you say that you know deeply that you are a fool, and if that is a reality, what should you do? You should not do anything. Because if you are a fool, the more you do, the more you spread your foolishness.

So, if you realize, "I am a fool," just do not do anything. Do not try to be spiritual. Just be. Just live, and it will happen. If you still think you are very smart because you know that you are a fool, then you try to do many things. If you are truly aware that you are foolish, then you should not be doing anything.

Just do what life demands out of you — just that much, and nothing else. Do not try to be aware, do not try to be spiritual, do not try to get to heaven, and do not try to reach out to anything, because since you are a fool, you will do stupid things.

When feminine minds come and sit in my presence, it is very simple for them to drop themselves and become a part of it. When I say 'feminine' mind, I am not referring to women. There are women who have very masculine minds. Similarly, there are men who have very feminine minds. The masculine in you, that is the logical dimension in you, will be very uncomfortable in my presence. It feels threatened all the time.

Maybe that is one reason why spirituality is over-populated with women – even in our situation right now, it is so (*Laughs*). This is because somewhere a man is unable to be a man with me. He feels impotent when he sits in my presence, because his whole stupid sense of manhood has come to him from his masculinity. Almost ninety percent of his manhood revolves around his masculinity. Sitting in my presence makes the strong man in him crumble, and if he is not aware, he will not like it.

But if he is aware, he sees that this is a big relief. The prison has been broken for him. But if he is not aware, then this looks like a threat, and at first he struggles and protests and tries to create barriers and runs away. But people will not allow all of these things to happen; the first thing they do is run away (*Laughs*).

Now if you want to transcend your limitations, first of all, you have to grow into receptivity. See, this is very significant, but unfortunately, it has been badly misinterpreted because there are fools who understand everything literally. When they say, God created the man first and much later the woman, it just means this: one has to *become* feminine. When I say feminine, I do not mean that you have to become feminine in the body. Feminine means receptivity; you have to become receptive.

If you take it literally, you are a fool. Definitely this world happened with man and woman together. If man came first and woman came later, it could not have happened. Definitely when the bugs came, when the insects came, they also came as male and female. It is not to be taken literally, but in terms of consciousness, it is true that man happened first. Man means strength, physical strength, survival. When your survival is under threat, man is supreme. Then there is no room for the feminine. At such times, you push the feminine to the corner, and make everything masculine, because when survival is under threat, everything becomes masculine, and it has to. Masculine is good for survival. But if you want to receive something more, you have to become feminine. I repeat, do not understand masculine and feminine as physical bodies.

So if you have to become receptive, the first thing for you to see is, "Oh, I'm being stupid"; only then you will listen. When you are in a state of, "I know I am smart, I know what I'm doing," will you listen to me? In that state, you do not listen to anybody. But the moment it just sinks into you, and not just in your mind that, "I am absolutely stupid. I do not know the beginning or the end of my life. I do not know the very basis of my existence" – then you are ready to listen.

In fact, you have not even experienced your existence. You have only felt the impressions of life upon yourself. You have not experienced your being, because only in your being there is presence and existence. The rest is just a happening.

So this step of seeing that "I am foolish" is a step towards receptivity. Now you say, "My wife is not willing to play games with me" – this is because you play for your survival. In your play you have to prove your manhood, otherwise you are lost. These days, women also have become equally stupid. That is different. But somebody who at that moment is feeling feminine will not play with you when you are playing for survival, because she survives by receiving, not by doing.

You also survive only by receiving, but you are not aware of it. Only because this breath is being received by this body, your survival is happening. If you become too much of a man and block your nostrils, as you have blocked everything else (*Laughs*) — every other opening you closed — your survival is finished. Your survival happens only with receptivity, but in your need to survive you are destroying the very basis of your survival.

If you just look at the activity of humankind, it is very visible, is it not? In the name of survival, development, the good life, are we not destroying this planet which is the very basis of our survival? This you are also doing to yourself as an individual. You are not just destroying the planet, the globe; you are destroying yourself as an individual, too.

In this context, I have to read you a poem.

The Dark One
When I first heard the sounds of
Darkness and silence meeting within me
The little mind argued for light
The virtue, the power, the beauty
Light, a brief happening could hold me not
The all-encompassing darkness drew me in

Darkness the infinite eternity
Dwarfs the happened, the happening and the yet to happen

Choosing the eternal
Darkness I became

The dark one that I am
The divine and the devil are but a small part
The divine I dispense with ease
If you meet the devil you better cease

So please deepen this awareness of being stupid. Do not try to be smart. When you see, "I am truly stupid", intelligence has descended upon you. It takes enormous intelligence for a person to see the stupidity of who he is. Only an idiot thinks that he is smart. An intelligent person is aware of his foolishness. Let it sink deeper so that you do not have to play a game to prove anything. Not even to yourself. You do not have to play a game to enhance your security, or to substantiate yourself. You only play a game to dissolve into it.

A game is a tool for you to dissolve into, not to prove who you are, not to establish yourself. But we have forgotten about the game. Instead, we are only pursuing victory. We are not playing a game. When you play like this nobody wants to play with you. Nobody, no sensible human being will want to play with you if your interest is only victory and not the game.

Just play, simply play, then there is no problem. You will see that play becomes a process of dissolution. It is victory, which makes your ego stand up, not the game. The game is always dissolving. It makes you merge into a certain process.

—◦◦◦◦—

"Presence cannot be practiced. It cannot be created. If you allow it, it will happen."

Questioner: Sadhguru, how can we practice your presence when you are not physically there?

Sadhguru: Presence cannot be practiced, it cannot be created. If you allow it, it will happen. So from the simple meditation that has been taught to you in the form of Shoonya, to everything else, it is just to bring you that sense of allowing – just learning to keep yourself aside.

The whole process of Isha Yoga is just that. Now do not hanker to feel somebody's presence, because then your mind will start creating things. Do not expect that something like this should happen. Then your mind will start dreaming and hallucinating.

You are always in the presence. It is just that for you to become aware of that, it takes a little more aliveness. If that aliveness has to happen, the rock that you have placed on it has to be rolled aside. The rock of ignorance is just how deeply you are identified with things that you are not.

"Now," you may ask, "on a day-to-day basis, when I am walking on the street, how do I feel it?" I want you to understand this. I do not want this presence to be used as a security. "Oh, that is not fair" you think, because they always taught you that God will save you, that he will hold your hand. The presence can be used in that sense, but that is a very limited way to use it. If you are a spiritual seeker, that is not the way. If you are still struggling with your own life then okay, you can use it that way. I do not want to deny that to you, but at the same time I do not want to encourage you into that kind of thing.

Feeling the presence truly means that it simply becomes your life breath. "How can I make it that way?" You cannot make it that way. If you make yourself less and less and less, the presence becomes more and more and more in your life. "How to make myself less than what I am right now?" Right now your life is revolving around you. It is all about you, is it not? So, the very device of accepting a guru in your life is this: suddenly your life no longer revolves around you. You are a secondary person in your life. You are not the hero in the drama. If suddenly somebody else is the main person in your life, and you are just a side role, then this presence becomes a living thing, like your life breath.

That sounds very enslaving. Logically, if you look at it, it is pure slavery, but experientially if you go into it, it is absolute liberation. I am in danger for expressing these things in language. The danger is always there, because if this is analyzed logically, it looks like somebody is slowly working to enslave you. Even before I uttered that word I knew, this is how it will be seen logically. But if you enter into that space, you will see it is absolute freedom.

"You are only polishing your ignorance. The shinier it becomes, the more dangerous it becomes, because you cannot grasp it anymore."

Questioner: Once the disciple has assimilated what is to be learnt into himself, what is the role of the guru? I know his presence is always there. In every breath his presence is there. But does this mean his physical presence is not necessary for more in-depth growth once this stage is reached?

Sadhguru: See, if you begin to feel this presence every moment of your life, then there is no question of "more in-depth." You have become absolute in that. So when you say, "when we are assimilating this knowledge into ourselves," the knowing and the knower are still separate, so that is ignorance.

As I said earlier, you are only polishing your ignorance. The shinier it becomes, the more dangerous it becomes, because you cannot grasp it anymore. When it was rough and crude you could have picked it up in your hands and seen, "Yes, this is my ignorance." When it becomes too smooth and shiny, then you know you have no grip over it. So, do not polish your ignorance. Do not come to these conclusions that you have assimilated this knowledge, because no knowledge was given to you. You have invented some knowledge. Isha Yoga is not knowledge. It is just a device.

You can employ the device, but you cannot store the device in your head. It is of no use.

With any device for that matter, you can only use it. For example you have a car. It is a good device to reach point A from point B. But now you have a 500 SL, not as a device to reach somewhere, but to enhance yourself. Now, this is burdensome. This is not a device anymore. This is a support for your ego. So whether it is 500 SL or Isha Yoga (*Laughs*), you can use it the same way. This will happen to everybody at some point.

"Oh, I got this. I got the point." When you say this it means you did not get it, because it is not something that you can get. If it is something that you can lose, then you truly exist. Otherwise you are just a small happening.

So with the knowledge of yoga, with the knowledge of gods and heavens and hells and religions and theologies, you are actually only becoming smaller. When I say that, you say, "No, no, in the last few years my understanding has improved. I have become bigger." That becoming bigger is making you smaller, I want you to understand.

How do you become bigger in life? Who is the big man in the town? The man who has got one billion bucks, is it not? That is the man you refer to as a big man — somebody who holds a certain amount of money, power, or position.

So your becoming bigger is only in terms of accumulation. Whether you accumulate diamonds, people, things, money, knowledge, it is all the same: it is just different ways of constructing your ego. What materials you use to construct varies from person to person, but you are always using external inputs to construct. That is not the purpose of yoga.

When we say 'self-knowledge', there is really no such thing, because 'self' is not something that you can know. See, what is it that you call 'myself'? I am sitting here. I am capable of seeing, hearing, all these things. This is 'myself', isn't it? So, the knower is 'myself', but what you are calling myself right now, in the immediate sense, is just the accumulation of knowledge and impressions upon this knower. So, however much you accumulate, still the knower keeps receding further and further. You are still only gathering objects; the subjectivity is missed.

In the yogic tradition there is a very wonderful story about a boy. You might not have heard of him, but in India there is almost nobody who would not have heard about him. There was a boy whose name was Satyakama. There is an elaborate story about this but I will not go into it now. Satyakama was born in a certain family of brahmins. Today the word 'brahmin' has just reduced itself into a certain caste, but fundamentally 'brahman' means the ultimate. A 'brahmin' means one who is in touch with the ultimate. Today somebody is a brahmin by birth; this does not mean anything. If you are a brahmin out of your awareness, that is everything.

So, this was a family of brahmins not only by birth; they truly existed as brahmins. This boy, when he reached twelve years of age, was sent to a certain master to study with him. You know India has such elaborate scriptures, handling every aspect of life, every kind of life science. Today when I say 'life sciences', it probably means biology. I do not mean it in that sense. I mean the science of what is truly needed for a person to live.

So, Satyakama went to the master. Twelve years he studied. Having been a brilliant boy, he grasped everything well -- all the Vedas, the Upanishads, the Brahma Sutras. These are what I am referring to when I say life sciences. They contain everything that can ever be said about a human being. Anything that can be said about man and the beyond is said in these scriptures. That is why they are so dangerous.

He learned everything in twelve years of study. Being a brilliant boy he grasped everything. After twelve years the master said, "There is nothing more for you to learn. You have learnt everything that is there to learn. I think it is better you go home."

The boy went back home. He entered the house. The father, who was sitting there, looked at him and said, "You have come back an ignorant fool."

"No, I learnt all the Vedas, the Upanishads. I can recite them backwards, if you want."

The father said, "I know that you have learnt everything that can be learnt. But that which learns, about that you have not learnt anything. From the very way you walk, I know you know too much. But you do not know that which knows, so you are very ignorant. We are true brahmins. We are not just brahmins by birth. If you want to be here you must know the knower, not that which can be known. You go back to your master."

The boy had come home after twelve years. He had just graduated. You are supposed to set up a party for him (*Laughs*), but this father just sends him out of the house.

The boy went back to the master and said, "My father says I am ignorant. I know all the Vedas, the Upanishads. Everything that you taught me I have learnt sincerely, but my father says I am ignorant. He says I must know the knower."

So the master said, "Oh, you want to know the knower. That is good. These twelve years you were only interested in that which can be learnt, so we taught all the nonsense that can be known learnt in the world. You learnt all that, so we sent you back. Now you are saying that you want to know the knower. Let me see. You do one thing, take this herd of cattle and go into the forest." There were four hundred cattle in the ashram. The master said, "Take the cattle and go into the forest and just be with them. When they become a thousand, you come back."

You know from four hundred to become a thousand, how much time it is going to take? But the master just said, "However much time it takes, when they become a thousand, you come back." Satyakama could not believe this. He had gone through the full scale of education. It was like you went to a university, studied for twenty years and got a PhD. Then you were told, "You have to be a cowboy.

(*Laughs*) You have to just graze cattle."

He went. Initially, there was turmoil and struggle, and he thought, "What is this? Everybody has rejected me. And now my master has given me this." For a few weeks and months the mind ran on. See, for your mind to run continuously, you need input; without fuel it cannot go on. Constantly you are giving that input, is it not?

But slowly, he forgot about what was happening in the ashram and at home. These Vedas, Upanishads, this knowledge is powerful, only if there is somebody to listen to you. All knowledge is powerful only if there is somebody to show it off to; otherwise the cows will not listen to your Vedas. They will just go chomp, chomp, chomp. So, slowly this chomp, chomp, chomp sank into him. These Vedas, these Upanishads, these twelve years of learning the scriptures, slowly they fell apart.

Over a period of time he just became like the cows. When he was hungry he ate, otherwise he just sat there. They say the shape of his eyes changed. They became like a cow's eyes. He became so much like the cow, but he now truly existed. He was no more a slave to his mind. When he sat, he sat absolutely. If he was with a cow, he was a cow. If he touched a tree, he became a tree. If he sat on the earth, he became the earth. He just became an absolute presence, because there was no input to the mind.

Then he forgot his language. He forgot his numbers. Then he did not know whether it was a thousand or ten thousand cows. He was simply there. Then the cows came to him one day and told him, "We are one thousand. Let us go back to the master."

So, he just went with the cows, back to the ashram. He just came, and all the cows entered the ashram and stood there. He also stood. The ashram had grown big; the number of disciples had multiplied manifold, and he just stood along with the cows.

Then all the disciples, full of excitement, came and said, "Satyakama has come back. Let us count the cows. Maybe he does not have a thousand. Let us see." They counted, and it was one thousand. Then they told the master, "It is a thousand. He has come back."

The master said, "No, it is not a thousand. It is a thousand and one, because Satyakama has completely lost his person now. He has just become an absolute presence."

So, do not make everything into an input. Do not keep gathering. From ancient times we have been gathering, is it not? Initially it was just food, and then lots of little things came. Now maybe it is stones, furs, this and that. Our ability to gather is enormous now. We gathered enough on this planet, and now we are going to gather things from other planets soon. But it does not matter how much you gather, you will not know the absolute. You will not know the ultimate. It is possible only when you throw away the gathering, when you can be here without anything .When I say 'without anything', it does not mean getting rid of something. It is just that, if all the impressions that you have gathered in the form of knowledge, are kept away, then

49

you will see that which knows everything. Then that which is the basis of knowing becomes present in a huge way. Huge is the wrong word, because it becomes absolute and unbounded.

The very word 'yoga' means union. You know this. It means you and the existence, you and the other, have become one. When this happens, it does not mean that 'that' becomes a part of you. It is just that you lost yourself. You lost yourself so you have become one. You cannot include 'that' as a part of you. That is an illusion. Only if you lose yourself, you can become one, not otherwise. This is dangerous talk, because nobody wants to lose himself. Everybody wants to find himself.

The whole effort in life is to find yourself, not to lose yourself. That is the reason why you take lifetimes. You want to go east, but you start heading towards west, so you need a full circle. These people who are bound west, you cannot suddenly turn them east, because the gold rush is in that direction, isn't it? (Laughs) The rush is in this direction, but the gold is in that direction. If I tell you to go the opposite way, it is like walking back into the ocean, which nobody wants to do. So generally we people run the full circle. But because they are trying to run this way and that, most of them do not have the necessary perseverance and energy to run the full circle.

But if you have trust, you will not have to run the full circle. With somebody's presence, with another being's presence, you can walk on the path. When the gold is here, if you walk the opposite way, you will be seen as an idiot. But you will dare to be an idiot only when there is trust in you.

—◦◦◦◦—

"You just see how to make your seeking the most important thing in your life, even bigger than your life. If you do that, the rest we will take care of."

Questioner: In our next lifetimes, when you have gone and we all just start walking west again, will there be support?

Sadhguru: (*Laughs*) Why are you postponing it? This has been expressed in many beautiful ways. So many sages in India have expressed this in such beautiful dialectical ways, but the logical minds — people who are trained in the process of logic — always misunderstand the dialectical language. So let me use an example that you understand better.

I do not know the exact words but, somewhere when somebody asked Jesus about Abraham, he said, "Before Abraham was, I am." We know on which date Jesus was born, and we know on which date he was crucified, but he said he was before people who were born centuries before him. Jesus was saying this because he was not talking about himself as a person. He was not ignorant: he knew that this body was born on a certain day, and was likely to end on a certain day. But as a possibility, as a consciousness, he said he was before Abraham also. So, in that context, I would say I am before Jesus also, before Krishna also.

So, do not worry about what to do in the 22nd or 23rd century. If somebody can be before, he will be after also. You do not worry about those problems now. Focus on what you need to do now. Because, whichever way you project logically, whichever way you logically understand, it is wrong, because it is not in the realm of logic. So whatever is said, it is bound to be misunderstood.

Above all, you sitting here with me, saying that you are seeking this intensely, and at the same time, you are saying, "After you are gone, in my next life, what?" That is an insult. (*Laughs*) Why I am saying this is an insult is that if you are really seeking, if your seeking is absolute, and if you do not attain it in this life, then it means it is due to my incapability, isn't it?

So you do not worry about the next life and what will happen after me. You just see how to make your seeking the most important thing in your life, even bigger than your life. If you do that, the rest we will take care of.

If your seeking is just one part of your life, we can only handle one part of your life. A little better life will happen. That is why I am always telling people when they want to come for Samyama, if all you want to do is live well — there is so much glorification about living your life well today in this culture — Isha Yoga and Bhava Spandana Program[1] is enough for you. Do not seek anything more. It is unnecessary, because you are stepping into a terrain that you are not ready for.

Only if you want to know the very source of life, if you are

[1] An intermediate – level spiritual program offered by Isha

not interested in just living a good life – if you have lived your life well and you are bored with it, and you want to know the very source, the very origin of life, the very beginning and beyond – only then you seek other processes. Otherwise, Isha Yoga and Bhava Spandana have enough tools to create a good life.

So if a longing has come within you that living your life well is not sufficient for you, you want to know, why the hell this life? You want to know what this life is and where it begins and where it goes, only then you explore other dimensions. If that longing has not come into you, do not waste your time trying to do other things. If that longing has become so intense that you are unable to sleep, that is good. It means you are getting somewhere. It has become so intense that nothing else is important. You want to know. If wanting to know has become enormous within you, much bigger than yourself and your life, then you make it very easy for me. But right now, my whole work is to bring that longing into you. Until now, my work has been just to bring the longing into you. If longing happens within you, then my work is very easy. I am good at that. This is your job, but I am doing your job also right now. (*Laughs*)

"Love must be an outpouring of who you are. It cannot be practiced."

Questioner: I want to go back and ask you to talk a little bit more about belief and faith. I do not know what faith is, but I understand belief. I do not know anything about spirituality. I do not even know that it exists. I do not know whether to believe you or disbelieve you. All I know is that I have love, even towards those who are hurtful, so...

Sadhguru: Why, one sure thing is, at least half a dozen times you said, I do not know, I do not know, I do not know.

Questioner: That is true, I do not know. I want to find out.

Sadhguru: So if you do not know, from where can you judge whether what I am saying is true or not? You cannot. So I want you to understand that. When you truly see the "I do not know," all judgment goes away from you. All prejudice goes away from you. Only in knowing something you can be prejudiced. Your knowledge is prejudice. Is it not so? When you are truly "I do not know," there is no prejudice in you, there is no judgment in you. You have just become a being.

This "I do not know" is slowly becoming deeper in the last four years for you. It is getting deeper. So deepen it faster. Reach the very root and see "I do not know that you are." Then the "I do not know" is not just in your head. Your whole being will say, "I do not know." Every cell in your body will say, "I do not know." Let it become like that. When it becomes like that, you are not judgmental. You are not judgmental simply because you are not attached to any particular prejudice.

And you are not attached to any particular prejudice simply

because your identifications with things and people around you have weakened. That is the only way. That is the process. The reason why somebody is free of prejudice is that his identifications are not too strong. The moment your identification is strong with something, you are naturally prejudiced towards that. Whether you are for it or against it, you naturally become prejudiced. So you said, "I do not know any spirituality." This is spirituality: to weaken the identification so that it slowly dissolves.

See, somebody robbed your house. Even though you are still alive, you say, "Someone robbed me." He only robbed the house, the contents in the house. But in your experience, if your identification with this house is very strong, you really feel that he robbed you.

Moreover, people are trying to teach you how to practice love and kindness. If you practice this, you will become sick. People who practice love are sick people. Love must be an outpouring of who you are. It cannot be practiced. If you are practicing it, it is just the currency that you are using to get what you have to get in your life. It is just the currency that you are using to cunningly squeeze things out of somebody else. You cannot practice it.

If you are not practicing, love can overflow from you. If it happens, it is very beautiful. But if you are practicing it, it cannot work. Now you cannot practice spirituality either. Doing whatever simple practices that you are doing, with these tools slowly your identifications have come to a point that even if somebody bombs you, you are not bursting with fury. You are still able to see things with sense: simply looking at things the way they are, without a reaction within you. That is fine. It is not everything, but it is good.

So, whatever devices you use, you are dissolving your identities. It is just that we have to hasten the arithmetic. Now, from multiplication we came down to addition, from addition we have come down to subtraction, from subtraction we have to come down to division. When we do sufficient division, then we have to settle down and see that the whole arithmetic springs from the big zero, isn't it?

So, when you experientially become a zero – zero means 'shoonya' – that is it. You like to walk the path step by step, and play the number game. It is good that, at least, you are walking in the right direction, not climbing upwards. You are stepping downwards. (*Laughs*) From multiplication we have come down a little bit. You were trying to multiply your life, but now you are subtracting things from your life. It is good. It is beginning to happen. That is the spiritual process.

"If you give a conscious expression to this deep longing for expansion within you, then we say it is a spiritual process."

Questioner: I want you to talk a little bit about desire.

Sadhguru: Desire?

Questioner: I had another car accident —

Sadhguru: It seems somebody offered you a ladder to heaven and you refused it... (Laughter)

Questioner: Yes, I think so.

Sadhguru: That is not it. That is being stupid. She was driving a car and somebody dropped a ladder in front of her. This was a ladder to heaven and she refused it. She tried to avoid it and hit something else.

Questioner: I thought I was turned the right way.

Sadhguru: If it happened on an interstate (Laughter), it would have been such a possibility. You know we said, "Yoga, the ladder to divinity."

Questioner: I know. Well, after I avoided the ladder, and I was at the hospital, and I realized that I didn't die, I was sad. I was sad about all the things that I knew I wanted to do with my life. I was most sad about singing and performing. I felt that was a gift that I had, and that I wanted to share. So I continue to struggle with that desire. Did God really give me this gift so that I should share it, or is that me and my ego still struggling? We have talked about desire, and in general for these past three years, the need to express that has lessened in terms of ego. It is not so much "Oh, I need to be big" and it feels more like wanting to share my gift.

Sadhguru: The world also needs a respite from your music, doesn't it? (*Laughs*) There is a joke that is making rounds in India. You know the school kids are talking about this everywhere. They have a list of the most corrupt people, who happened to be on a holiday cruise in the Indian Ocean. Now the ship started sinking. They wondered among these twelve most corrupt, who would be saved. People started guessing that maybe it will be this person, maybe that person, because of this reason, that reason. Then the kids said, "No, India is saved." (*Laughter*)

In many ways so is desire. It is just that we are not using that word. Desire is just an anxiety to enhance yourself. Whether the desire is to acquire money, things, or people, or to do something, the desire is just an anxiety to enhance oneself.

Why do you have a need to enhance yourself? It is because somewhere there is a strong and constant feeling of inadequacy. Unfortunately, 99% of human activity is coming from this inadequacy. So man has to enhance himself with activity. He has to do something. So, desire is just that.

Why has this desire come? I think we have looked at this many times. The desire has again sprung up from the wrong identifications, because you are identified with the limited. The energy, which you call 'life', is trying to find its original nature of unboundedness. Therefore, it desires. But because you are unconscious, you keep desiring things and activities, this and that, and with this much experience in life, you know that if you satisfy one desire, the next one is right there ready to spring up. Yes?

So let us look at desire in terms of money, property, power, wealth or whatever else. If you look at it this way, you will see that once one thing is satisfied, desire seeks the next, and the next, and the next. So, if you just stop and look at how your desire is progressing, you will see that your desire will never be satisfied with anything.

Your desire is seeking to grow. With how much will it be satisfied? It wants to become unbounded. If you just stop and look at your desire, it becomes very clear. Desire is unconsciously trying to push you toward your unbound-edness. Because somewhere this unbounded nature got identified with the limited body, from then on desire is constantly working to take you towards the unbounded. So, all the desires that come up within you are expressions for this longing to become unbounded. But it is done through limited physical dimensions. It may be money, wealth, jewels, or it may be singing or whatever else.

But it does not matter how much you do or how much you gather. Physical things and physical activity can never take you to the unbounded. The physical is always limited, isn't it? It can become big but it cannot become unbounded.

So this energy is seeking to reach towards its unboundedness, but you are offering a physical possibility. This is a spiritual process, but with a dead end. It cannot get you anywhere, but at the same time it keeps you constantly running. At every point in your life it makes you believe, this is it. But the moment that is fulfilled, you know that is not it. There is the next one and the next one and the next one.

So if you bring awareness to the process of desire, if you bring awareness to the mechanism of desire, to the way it is functioning within you, you will see your desire is only about becoming limitless. If you give a conscious expression to this deep longing for expansion within you, then we say it is a spiritual process.

Fundamentally, desire is a spiritual process. Unfortunately, it is finding an unconscious expression. If it is finding unconscious expression through things and activities, we say it is a materialistic process. Please give it a conscious expression. Instantly you will know, "It is not this or that that I desire, I want to become unbounded. I am not going to settle for this much or that much."

Maybe by the time you are fifty or sixty, you will be tired and you will settle for this much. That is different. Settling for something is different, but you are not fulfilled with that, isn't it? Because energy will never be fulfilled until it finds its original nature.

"The necessary awareness is absent. That is why the fear of death exists."

Questioner: Earlier you mentioned that we are always courting death. I just want you to talk a little more about why we are so afraid of death, and how that is manifested in our lives.

Sadhguru: Now these are two different aspects that you are putting together. When I said you are courting death, I meant that it is the fear of life which makes you court death. Seeking security is courting death. When people feel insecure they will just curl up into a foetal position and sleep; have you noticed this? The need is to go back into the womb. The womb is not really in the mother. The womb is really in death, please see. The physical mother is just a small manifestation of that, but the real womb is in death.

When people feel insecure they want to drink and sleep, because sleep is just a small manifestation of death. People want to sleep absolutely like a log because it gives them freedom from life. This whole courting death thing has come because of the need to seek security. From where did the insecurity spring up, first of all?

Insecurity comes to you because you feel like a little person in this vast existence. If you look around, you do not know where it begins, where it ends. So fear and insecurity are very natural.

So once again everything comes down to your limited identifications. You identify yourself as a body only because of that. First of all, you are creating a distinction between life and death. Otherwise life and death are just whatever you are referring to as 'life', which is being born as an infant and becoming an adult, growing old, and one day being gone. So that is life, is it not? That and what you are referring to as death are both just small happenings in the infinite possibility which I am referring to as life. If you wish you can call it death. You know both ways, it is okay. But you have an allergy to the word 'death'; you would prefer to call it 'life'.

You have always associated the words 'darkness', 'death', 'devil' with evil. But if you want to know life, there is no other way to know it except by fully coming to terms with and accepting death. Only that person who is willing to die can live. If you do not want to die you should not live. It is as simple as that.

So they are not really separate. The separation has come out of ignorance. The separation has come because first of all you have separated yourself from life. Because of that all the other separations have come. The whole range of dualities has sprung up in life simply because you separated yourself from the rest of existence by identifying yourself with the limited form. From there every other duality has come. That is the basis.

So fear of death is just another manifestation of it. It is just pure ignorance because you are identified with the limited form. Your whole life is about protecting the limited form.

You have come with certain deep instincts to protect the limited form. The necessary awareness to look beyond, to rise beyond this, is absent. That is the only reason why the fear of death exists.

PART TWO

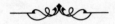

CONNECTION:

Relationships, Suffering Mind, Emotion

"Relationships are necessary to exist in the world; whether you keep them beautiful, or ugly, is all the choice that you have."

There are various types of relationships that you hold in your life. There is a relationship with a neighbor, with a friend, with a wife, with a husband, with a child; with parents; with siblings; there are so many. There are lovers' relationships; there are even relationships between people who hate each other — everything is a relationship.

Fundamentally, all relationships in your life have come up medical help. When you yelled at your wife, they thought it was normal. (*Laughs*) When you yell at your boss everybody knows you need medical help. So they take you to a doctor. Initially, the doctor tries to talk you out of it, but you will not budge. Then the next thing he does is put a pill into you.

It is because our lives have many complex activities that we have various types of relationships. There are various levels of involvement with different types of people on a day-to-day basis. We are constantly shifting from one type of relationship to another. This moment you are on the phone with your business partner; the next moment you are talking to your wife; then the next moment you are talking to your child or to your neighbor. Life is like that. You cannot just tune yourself to one thing and say: "Okay, right now I am going to be only like this." It is constantly changing.

Now because of the complexity of this adjustment that you have to make, if you treat your wife like you treat your business partner, immediately you are in trouble. If you treat your business partner like you treat your wife, then again you are in trouble. Isn't it so? If you treat your child like your husband, you are in trouble. If you treat your husband like your child, then again you are in trouble. So it is something that needs constant juggling; in life you need to do quite a bit of juggling to keep these relationships going.

So it all depends on how many balls you picked up for juggling. If you just had one ball, it would have been easy. But if you have picked up ten, now juggling is complex. You do not want to drop any one of them. That is the whole problem. If you want to drop eight of them and just take two and juggle, that would be easy, but you do not want to drop any one of them because if any one of them falls, a part of your life will fall apart. You want to juggle all the ten balls at the same time.

When you are doing this juggling, you cannot focus on anything else in your life, isn't it? When you have ten balls to juggle, can you think of anything else? You cannot think of anything else because the juggling needs to be on all the time. Even for one moment you cannot put it down. So these relationships come from a certain compulsion in you, because without fulfilling these relationships you will be nothing.

There is another way to exist; one can exist without any relationships. One is so complete within himself that it does not matter. But right now the quality of your relationships decides the quality of your life. It is definitely deciding the quality of your life.

So, how does one have the most beautiful relationship? It does not matter whether it is in the office, in the home, on the street, or anywhere else. How can we have the most beautiful possible relationship every moment of our lives, wherever we may be?

The basis of our relationship comes from a certain need. If you look at it, you are trying to somehow make yourself happy by building different types of relationships by doing different types of activities. Isn't it so? You make friendships, you get married, you have children, you start businesses, and you do everything because somewhere you believe this will bring you happiness.

So somewhere in pursuit of happiness, we built all these relationships. Or in other words, somewhere we try to squeeze some happiness out of people; somehow, we try to get some happiness out of somebody who is next to us right now. Once you do this, relationships will be constant trouble. Without relationships you cannot do; with them you cannot do either... (*Laughs*)

This is something that I see all the time. Generally, for most people, the closest relationship that they know is the man-woman relationship. Here is what you find: if they are together they are quarrelling. If you put them apart for twenty-four hours they cannot be without each other. If you put them together, in ten minutes again they will be back to the same thing. (*Laughs*) So you cannot be without the person; you cannot be with the person. This is trouble, isn't it?

This happens because your relationship comes from a certain need within you. There is no sense of joy or happiness within you; you are trying to extract it from somebody and that person is trying to extract it from you. Now, this is bound to become a battle; but we have come to an agreement that we will not bomb each other to death; we will just torture each other in so many different ways. It is an agreement; we will not finish each other off, because if I finish you off, what will I do without you? (*Laughs*)

So, if relationships have to be really beautiful, it is very important that a human being turns inward and looks at himself before he looks at somebody else. Before you look at somebody else, it is very important that you look at yourself in a very deep way. If you become a source of joy by yourself, and your relationships are about sharing your joy, not squeezing joy out of somebody, then you would have wonderful relationships with everybody.

Is there anybody in the world who would have any problems with you if you were going to share your joy with them? But if you are only trying to extract joy from them, then that is where the problem is. Relationships have become a problem because we are not using them to enhance our lives. We are trying to fill the gaps in our lives with relationships. If you are very happy, you have a need to share your joy with somebody. If you are unhappy, then also you need somebody to share your misery with.

See, today if you go on the street and watch, you see every minute, hundreds of people passing by. But how many truly joyful faces do you see? Very few. If you see any, usually they are very young faces. People over thirty, all have long faces. What has happened to them? For most of them, their lives have worked out far better than they ever imagined. Materially, are you all not living far better than your fathers and grandfathers? Are you not? Almost every one of you is living better than your grandfathers – unless your grandfather was a king. So, it is not that something has gone wrong with your lives. But still you carry long faces!

Some time ago I was speaking to a group of people at Princeton University, and I asked, what has happened to people over thirty? Are they all carrying long faces because it is an international phenomenon? This is not limited to any particular place. (Laughs) One lady stood up and said, "They are all married!"

If people are getting married to multiply their joy, that is wonderful. But if people are getting married to multiply their misery, that is not okay. So, if your relationships are about sharing your joy with people around you, then there would be no problem with it. If your relationship is about extracting something out of somebody, there will be constant trouble. It does not matter how well you manage it, there will be constant trouble. Even if you have an MBA, it will not help. If you have an MBA, does it help you at home? You see, even though you are a great manager of many things outside, your relationships are still a mess. If your relationship was an offering to the person who is next to you right now, then everything would be fantastic.

On the physical level, we are all obviously interdependent. But in terms of your experience, you need not be interdependent. You can be an absolute experience by yourself. The whole world is miserable, but you can still be joyful within yourself. This possibility is always there. It all depends on whether your inner experiences are enslaved or mortgaged to external situations or not.

For example, probably nobody here is old enough for this, but if you bought a car in the 1940s, along with the car you had to get yourself two servants, because in the morning you would need a 'push start'. In the 1950s, if you got a car, one servant would do, because it became 'crank start'. Today all your cars are 'self-start', isn't it? Is it not time that you put a 'self-start' on your happiness? I am just talking about upgrading technologies. (*Laughs*) Is it not time? But right now your relationships are just on 'push start'. Somebody has to get it going every day for you; otherwise, you will feel down.

If your happiness and your joyfulness were on 'self-start', then you would have fantastic relationships with everybody around you. Please look at your own life and tell me, would you like to live and work with people who are joyful or miserable? Joyful, isn't it? I want you to please remember, everybody wants the same thing. So if you are truly a joyful person, everybody wants to have a relationship with you. There is no hassle about that; nobody wants to be away from you. The only reason why people who told you just yesterday they love you very much, want to keep a distance from you today is because you want to extract joy from them. It does not work like that.

So, you have formed relationships, after all, because in life people are interdependent in so many ways. You cannot be handling every aspect of your life yourself. You need people around you. That is why you need relationships; and people are willing to be around you only if you want to offer something to them. If you want to take something from them, everybody is very self-defensive with you. Please see, the closest people around in your life are more defensive with you than with somebody else on the street. How unfortunate. Whenever we have a program going on, if something comes up where people want to share their thoughts and experience, they say, "No, my relative is here, I cannot share." If some stranger is there, they will share.

You have more layers of resistance with people who are close to you than with people you do not know. This is unfortunate. Is it not so? You should have broken the barriers you built with people whom you know, and it should have been very easy to be with them, but that is not how it is. With people whom you know, you have to be extremely cautious. With strangers you are okay. Because once you set up a relationship where you are trying to extract, there is so much self-defensiveness about the whole thing. Constantly people start building forts around themselves to protect themselves from others. So, you cannot be without each other, and at the same time you cannot be with each other; that is what happens to relationships.

Relationships are necessary for you to exist in the world. Whether you keep them beautiful or ugly is all the choice that you have. You have no choice about not having any relationship. There is no choice. Maybe you do not get married, or maybe you do not build a family. But still you have relationships with anything and everything around you. So the choice is just this: either you make a relationship beautiful or ugly; that is all the choice you have. Make it very pleasant or unpleasant; that is all the choice you have.

If you had a choice between pleasantness and unpleasantness, between joy and misery, between beauty and ugliness, what would you choose? Definitely joy, is it not? Definitely, pleasantness. But why does unpleasantness happen? Why is misery happening? Simply because nothing about you is in control; everything is happening accidentally.

Let us look at this: what are the things which you call 'myself' right now?

Questioner: Ego.

Sadhguru: What is this ego? Where is your ego? The nasty part of you is what you call ego. It is just you — when you turn nasty, you call it ego. (*Laughs*)

There is no ego; it is just you. Sometimes you are pleasant, sometimes you are unpleasant — that is your nature. You do not know how to hold one particular quality. It all depends upon the situations in which you exist. If outside situations turn nasty, you also become nasty and you call this your ego. It is not your ego; it is just you turning nasty. What are the things which you call 'myself?

Questioner: Body.

Sadhguru: Definitely body. What else?

Questioner: Mind.

Sadhguru: Your mind, yes.

Questioner: Emotions.

Sadhguru: Yes, emotions.

Questioner: Relationships.

Sadhguru: That is not you; that is yours. Do you call your relationships 'myself'? No. Your body, your mind, your emotions, these three things are true. There is one more thing, even if it is not in your experience: the energy that makes all this happen, is also you. So your physical body, your mind, your emotions and your energy — all these are what you call 'myself'. The rest of the things — these egos, souls, atmans, paramatmans — are just stories that you heard. In your experience they are not there, isn't it?

It does not matter who told the story; it is not yet in your experience. In your experience, these are the only four realities. These four realities, unless they function the way you want them, nothing will happen in your life by intent; everything will happen by accident. If your physical body does not behave the way you want it to behave, physically you are accidental. If your mind does not behave the way you want it to behave, mentally, psychologically, you are accidental.

The same goes for emotions, and the same goes for energy. Right now, please closely examine yourself and see; how much of your body, how much of your mind, how much of your emotions, and how much of your energy is happening the way you want it? Very little. Right now, your mind, your emotions, your energy, and your body are mostly happening the way external situations demand, not the way you want them.

If the outside situations are pleasant, you also become pleasant. If outside situations are unpleasant, you also become unpleasant. So, who you are is very deeply enslaved to the situations in which you exist. Right now, if somebody tells you when you should get up, when you should lie down, what you should eat, what you should wear, you would consider this slavery. Is it not so? But right now somebody else is deciding how you will be within yourself. Whether you will be happy or unhappy is decided by somebody else. Is this not a most horrible form of slavery?

So you have no relationships; you are enslaved to things around you. A relationship is possible only when there is some sense of freedom within you as to who you are. For now this is just slavery; this is compulsiveness. Physical compulsiveness is leading you to certain types of relationships. Emotional compulsiveness is leading you to certain other types of relationships. Psychological compulsiveness is leading to some other types of relationships. It is coming from a deep sense of compulsiveness. When you exist here as a compulsive being, you cannot operate as a conscious being. Once there is no conscious way of existence, what you want will not happen. Whichever way situations ensue, that is the way your life will happen; you become accidental. Once you exist here as an accident, you are a potential calamity.

Right now, although for most people initially relationships bring joy, after that they bring only anxiety. Your enemies do not come and kill you. It is your loved ones, with whom you created relationships with lots of care, and which you always wanted — they are taking your life away. If your enemies come and take your life, there is some meaning to it, but it is your loved ones who are taking your life away. This is not okay. Somewhere we have not gotten the fundamentals right. This has happened because relationships have come out of compulsiveness, and not out of choice or out of consciousness.

Earlier someone asked what about the divine. This is yet another relationship; because you cannot get along with anybody in this world, you hold a relationship with God, and you twist and turn him around whichever way you want. Some people come and tell me, "God loves us." Especially in the West this is a big thing — "God loves me." I tell them, "The way you are only God can love you." (*Laughs*) Who else can love you, the way you are? If you are such that everybody cannot help but love you, that is a wonderful way to exist. God loves you; what does it mean? It does not mean anything. Simply because you are shit-scared of life, you want to imagine that God loves you. You do not like all this? It does not matter whether you like it or not; that is the truth. If you do not face it, there is no evolution in you. All you will know is solace. You will not know liberation and life.

So a relationship is possible only if you are an individual by yourself; only then you can hold a relationship. Otherwise, if it is coming from a compulsion, it is not really a relationship. Because of compulsive needs, you hang onto somebody. This is not a relationship; this is just clinging, because you will cling to anything actually. Please see this. You would actually cling to anything. Right now it happens to be human beings; or with some people it happens to be lots of dogs. (*Laughs*)

If one wants to have absolutely fantastic relationships, no matter where he goes, first he needs to establish himself as a joyful human being, somebody whose joy is on 'self start' not on 'push start'. If by himself he is fine, wherever he goes, he will have wonderful relationships with people. When you are not fine by yourself, you use the other person to fill in the gap; then you will be in constant trouble.

"Surrender is not an act. Surrender is a certain quality."

Questioner: Can we take the devotion and surrender that we feel towards any person or thing in our life, dissolve into it and become one with it? Or do we have to necessarily route our devotion through a spiritual teacher?

Sadhguru: If you surrender to somebody, you will only become a slave. You will not become free. Surrender is not an act. Surrender is a certain quality. When we talk about surrender, do not ever think I am talking about you surrendering to me. No, I do not want such an indignity to happen to you. (*Laughs*) It is not about you surrendering to me. It is about you becoming surrender. I am just a catalyst to bring about that quality in you.

So the question is instead of surrendering to somebody who

is a spiritual teacher or whatever you consider to be God, or the son of God, or a guru, you ask "Can I surrender to my husband? Can I surrender to my boyfriend? Can I surrender to my something else?"

No, you cannot surrender to anybody, because you cannot. You can create deceptions of surrender. Surrender is not something that you do. When you lose your will, you become surrender. Surrender is like an absence. You cannot create an absence.

See, you can create light, but can you create darkness? Switch off the light. Darkness has always been. So surrender is just that, just collapsing into the existence. It is not something that you do. When all your doings stop, you are surrender. When you do Shoonya, you are actually in surrender. If that is not there, there is no Shoonya, please see. Meditation is deep surrender. If you really become meditative, you are in surrender.

Surrender is just like darkness. It always is. It is not something that you do. Whatever you do is just a brief happening. Whatever you do is like a wave which comes and goes away, but it is not the ocean. The ocean is always there. It is the wave which is rising and receding.

So everything that you do is of a limited sphere. It happens and recedes. It happens with great relevance and loses its relevance after some time. Do you see how various things in your life were relevant at one point and how irrelevant they are right now? From the teddy bear to I do not know all that you have extended it to now (*Laughs*), it has

78

happened, has it not?

So everything that you do is like this. It is just a small, brief happening. So surrender is to break this cycle of little happenings and to fall back into the vastness, into the boundlessness of what life is. It is not something that you do with this person or that person. It is something that you become. It is a quality.

—◦◦◦◦—

"The attachment is not to somebody. This must be clearly understood. The attachment is to your body."

Questioner: Can I attain while being in a relationship, a marital-type relationship, a relationship that most people get very attached to? Is it possible to attain liberation while remaining in that kind of relationship?

Sadhguru: Divorce, divorce! (*Laughter*) I am joking. Now in any relationship there is attachment. Most people know relationships only as attachments. Sex-based relationships breed much more attachment.

Why it breeds much more attachment is that — and we have been again and again going back to this — the foundations of this ignorance, of this whole illusion is rooted in your identification with the body. Now where this body is involved between two people, there this attachment always deepens.

You know one dimension on the spiritual path is

brahmacharya or people not getting into these kinds of relationships. This is not because we are against relationships, not because we are against the biology of life, but because it deepens this attachment.

Now the attachment is not to somebody. This must be clearly understood. The attachment is to your body. Because you are deeply attached to this body you get attached to somebody. If you had no attachment to this body, you cannot get attached to anybody. Please see that.

So you do not have to work on your attachments with people around you. You really need to work on your attachment to your own body. As you release yourself from this, you are free from everything.

Now what kind of relationships you hold in your life, in one sense, is irrelevant. But its relevance is in whether we want to create a supportive situation for ourselves or not. In that way it could vary from person to person. Some people need this kind of relationship to ground them a little bit. Otherwise they would be too disturbed to seek anything in their life. They would not be seeking anything at all. Their whole life they would be struggling with themselves. So in a way, the wife will ground you. (*Laughs*) I am not insulting you, but if you are trying to take off and fly here and there, she will ground you a little bit.

If you are capable of flying, it is beautiful. When you are not capable of flying, if you are not grounded, you will be lost. So it is a kind of grounding. It holds you down.

In one way, if you look at it, it is a reverse process, but right now it could be useful to you, depending upon what stage of life you are in. When you are young, your identification with the body is very, very strong. As your body becomes creaky and when you look at it, it does not inspire you, and you know it is not going to inspire anybody else (*Laughter*), then you start identifying yourself with something else.

Please see, when you are in a certain age-group, your identification with the body is very strong. You are very much a body. By the time you are thirty-five, forty, you try to shift your identity to your mind and your emotions because you are not so strong in your body. It is no more a great thing. It is slowly receding. It is going towards death. Whether you are consciously aware of it or not, life is telling you in many ways that this body is slowly sliding into the grave.

Now you slowly build other defense mechanisms and survival techniques. You are trying to shift your attachment to your ideologies, to your philosophies, your likes, your dislikes, your emotions. When you are young, you seek physical freedom. When you become thirty-five, forty, you start saying, "Oh, that is foolish. The emotions are important. What we share between us is important." But when you are just eighteen, this is not what you want. You want physical freedom. (*Laughs*)

As you get older, you will see these emotions are too entangling and you do not like that. You want to shift your attachment to God, because everybody else has forsaken you by then (*Laughter*) and you are beginning to realize the ways of the world. So you look up to God.

All this is a basic survival instinct in you. You just try to hold this, and when that becomes weak, you hold the next one. When that becomes weak, you do not know where to go. When death comes, you will see, only fear is left with people. Their body becomes unimportant. Their philosophies become unimportant. Their emotions and other things become unimportant. Their gods also will disappear. Though somebody else will be repeating god's name to them, they themselves will only shake in fear and terror, till death comes, till the last moments come.

In India when people are about to die, they say you should not utter anything except god's name. This is something you notice. On a warm sunny day, if people go and get into the river, it is nice, they enjoy the water. On cold mornings they go and get into the river because they believe they must have a bath before they go to the temple. Then they say, "Shiva shivaaahhhh." Shiva has become a device to hang on to, to avoid the discomfort of life, which right now is the physical discomfort. God is just a device to avoid the discomforts of life. It is just a survival technique, nothing spiritual about it. There is no divine aspiration in it. "No, no, but I want to go to heaven and be with God." This is also a survival technique. All that you are seeking is to be well.

Now, being well means to be happy, is it not? Somebody has told you if you go to heaven, you will be very happy. That is why you want to get there. If they had told you that if you go to heaven, you will be eternally miserable, you would not want to go there. So it is not heaven that you are seeking. It is happiness. But as usual you are not straight about it; you are devious about what you are seeking.

So right now you are seeking a certain relationship. I want you to look straight at it. Why are you seeking it? Do not give it all kinds of meanings which do not exist. You seek a relationship because you have a physical need. You are seeking it because by yourself you are lost. You are seeking it because psychologically, emotionally, you need support. You are seeking it because that is the only way you know how to handle your fears and struggles within yourself.

You know very well, because at least in this country, you have enough experience behind you. You know, you have had these kinds of relationships – probably one, two, five, or ten – and you know very well, externally it creates only more struggle and conflict. But because you do not know how to handle your interiority, you are using the exterior to handle your interior.

That will only be a stop-gap arrangement. It will never work forever for anybody. It cannot. Now the very process of sexuality is biology, reproduction. If you look at the world biologically, all that you will see is that the whole world is simply reproduction, nothing else. The flowers are blooming, and somebody wants to write poetry about the romance of flowers blooming, but the flowers are just seeking to reproduce their own kind. Is it not so? Their colors, their fragrance are just two tricks to reproduce. If you look at the world biologically, everything is just plain reproduction. You are also just reproduction. If you simply look at yourself as a physical body, the only longing that is there in you is simply to reproduce. This is nature's trick to perpetuate life. Otherwise if you did not have this, this race would end tomorrow, isn't it?

Now you are using this basic instinct within you to reproduce in so many ways and you are giving it all kinds of meanings, which do not really exist. It is just that you have exposed your body to somebody and you think that is closeness. Somewhere you have shared certain things with somebody, which you cannot share with anybody and everybody on the street. This is because your religions, your cultures, your morals have brought a certain sense of shame and a certain sense of impurity into the basic biological process of life. It has become a way of opening up to a certain person, because the only thing that you are capable of opening up to somebody is your body, unfortunately. That is the highest opening that people are able to offer each other. The biggest thing that they can offer is opening their bodies to each other. Nothing more is happening.

The secret between them is that they have opened their bodies to each other. They have a kind of nucleus between them. It is a conspiracy. (*Laughs*) It is a certain kind of conspiracy that they have, that they cannot share with anybody else. If you share it with somebody else, there is going to be a fight, isn't it? The nucleus is going to break.

So this is the highest opening people know, and it is unfortunate. You can open yourself in a much deeper way, but it does not matter. Right now when you exist as a body, that is all you know and that is all you can do. It is fine. I am not against it, but it is not enough. You will never be satisfied with it. You will never be fulfilled with it.

If you want to experiment for a lifetime and then discover, it is up to you. If you have any intelligence you must discover today that this will not be fulfilling. This will only be managing life at a certain level. It will not be liberating. It will not be fulfilling in the true sense, and to manage this, how many deceptions you have to play! Things that you could easily share with some stranger you cannot share in the closest relationship. That is what has happened to most people.

I see, especially in India, not so much here, when people attend the Bhava Spandana Program, they want to share something. When they find a partner they say, "No, this is my relative. I cannot share with him." Your relative is supposed to be closer to you than anybody else. It is a blood relation, so with him you must be able to share everything, but "No, with a stranger I can share, but if my husband or wife is there, I cannot open my mouth." (*Laughs*)

So the closeness is only in one way. As I said, it is a conspiracy that they share. Everybody knows this stupid conspiracy, but everybody pretends as if it is a great conspiracy. (*Laughs*) Everybody knows but everybody pretends as if it is something else.

Those relationships have got nothing to do with your spiritual process. Spirituality is something that you do within yourself. How you want to manage your outside is left to you, but as the internal changes, it will naturally show in the exterior also. But if you want to manage a certain level of exteriority and you want to keep a certain thing going, it is up to you. What you do with your outside, I do not want to decide.

You do anything you want but please understand that for every single action that you perform, there is a consequence. If you can joyously accept the consequence, you do anything you want. If when the consequence of your action comes, you are going to cry, then you have no business doing those things.

If you know the bliss of marriage today, the pain of marriage will come tomorrow. It may come in so many ways. It may come in the form of death. It may come in the form of a child. It may come in the form of disease, or your wife may just start bitching so much. It may come in any way, but it will come in some way. Like the fear of losing. Nothing need to go wrong, just the fear of losing, that itself is very painful, is it not? Please understand, in this world whatever you do, for every action that you perform, there is a consequence. If you are an intelligent person, before you perform the action, you see the consequence. If you can joyously accept it, do anything you want. Have ten marriages. I have no problem.

But if you are the kind of person who does something tomorrow and when the consequence comes you cry, please look at it. Look at it carefully.

—◦⁊ɛ⁊◦—

"Not being identified does not mean not being involved. It just means not being entangled."

Questioner: We were talking about the process of dis-identification earlier. I wonder if you can talk a little bit about how one continues to function in the world as a lay person, while having this process of disillusion and dis-identification going on.

Sadhguru: Now you are talking about how to avoid disillusionment, but I actually want to disillusion you. The very spiritual process is to disillusion you in order to break all your illusions. People always say they do not want to be disillusioned, so they seek ignorance. I want to disillusion you. I hope life disillusions you as quickly as possible; I hope people around you disillusion you as quickly as possible. I hope they will not take a whole lifetime to do it. (*Laughs*)

If people around you keep you in your illusions for a very long time, then maybe by the time you realize that these comfortable illusions are not really getting you anywhere, your life will be over. What does disillusionment mean, after all? As far as you are concerned, somebody refused to fulfill your expectations, isn't it? And that is all the disillusionment you have. Disillusionment is good for you.

Now 'dis-identification' is different. In fact, illusion is just identification. All illusions have come to you only because of your identifications. The moment you think somebody is your husband, you are identified with him. Once you are identified, so many illusions grow about this person, which is humanly impossible for anybody to fulfill. So you have woven many illusions around this person. And when that person does not live up to your illusions, you are disillusioned.

Not being identified does not mean not being involved. It just means not being entangled. Being dis-identified gives you absolute freedom to throw yourself into life and do whatever you wish to do with it.

When you are identified you can do only certain things, please see. Look at your relationships. If somebody does a little more, it will hurt, if they do a little less, it will hurt. They are supposed to do just that much. (*Laughter*) It is like a scientific measurement – 'just that much'. Just that many ounces of everything, isn't it?

This is a sure way to destroy yourself. I hope life disillusions you quickly. If you do not give life an opportunity, I would like to. (*Laughs*)

"Stress is a part of life only if you have lost your sanity."

Questioner: Is celebration important in life?

Sadhguru: Life is celebration. If you are happy, every step

that you take and every breath that you take is a celebration. Have you noticed at a certain moment when you are very happy, every little thing that you do is a celebration? Only when you do not know joy, celebration has to be organized. Otherwise every moment of your life, whatever you do is a form of celebration. When you are very happy, just walking is a celebration. That is how it should be. Celebration need not necessarily mean we all have to get together and do something. Not necessarily. If individuals are happy, their very existence and their very life is a celebration; then if they come together, whether there is a party or otherwise, celebration will happen anyway.

When you meet your old friend, you are really happy, and over a glass of water you can have a great celebration. So the question is not about what you are drinking, what you are eating, what kind of atmosphere you are in; it is about whether you are joyful. It is the inner atmosphere which decides the celebration, not the external.

If there is no inner celebration and there is too much external celebration, you will become absolutely depressed. Right now, internally you are very down, and outside a big celebration is going on. You see, it becomes all the more difficult for you to enjoy these celebrations. At least if it was a normal situation, your depression could be easier to handle. Now with the big celebration outside, it becomes extremely difficult for you.

So celebration is not because we have a band, or we drink, or we eat, or we do something; celebration is because you are joyful. There is no other way for celebration. Right now somebody beats the drums, somebody dances, somebody sings, somebody eats, somebody drinks; why? They are somehow trying to get themselves into a joyful situation.

I am sure you definitely have had moments of joy in your life. When you were joyful, did the joy rain upon you, or did it blossom within and find an external expression? Which way was it? From within, or from the outside? Where did it happen?

It always came from within, but the only thing is, right now the ignition is outside. The start button is somewhere in somebody else's hand, not in your hand; but the joy is always within you, is it not? Did you ever feel joy from outside? Never. See, people talk about giving happiness and receiving happiness. This is all plain nonsense. You cannot give happiness, and, you cannot receive it. It is just that somebody's presence may ignite your happiness, but you do not receive happiness from anybody. You are unhappy, and if there is somebody who is very happy it may even become insulting rather than igniting.

So, if life has to become a celebration, one has to become absolutely joyful within oneself. "Is such a thing possible? Is this some empty talk? Do you know the realities of life? Maybe you come from some ashram where everything is perfect..." This is not empty talk.

Most of you are managing your own businesses and industries, we are also managing a large institution; over a quarter million volunteers around the world do various types of activities. See, working with volunteers is different. If you are managing businesses and industries, one of the main tools of your management is that if somebody does not function the way he should function, you fire him. That is the main tool of your management. We do not have that tool. I cannot fire anybody because everybody is a volunteer. (*Laughs*) It does not matter what they do, you cannot fire them. Do you know now how difficult management is? If any of you know what daily crisis is, I want to tell you, I see ten times more of that kind of crisis every day.

It is not because life situations are this way or that way that you are happy or unhappy. Somebody is happy not because everything is perfect with his life; somebody is happy because he is happy, that is all. So what is the difference? Why is it that some people seem to be happy and some people do not?

When you were just five years of age, you were simply happy by your own nature; somebody had to make you unhappy at that time. But now, at the present time, somebody has to make you happy. You just reversed the whole equation of life somewhere. If you were that happy when you were five years of age, by the time you were thirty, you should have become ecstatic, is it not? But just the reverse has happened for most people, and for most of you, life has worked out far better than you ever imagined. In spite of that, your happiness has not hit its peak.

If you look at yourself as a generation of people, never before has another generation known these kinds of comforts and these kinds of conveniences in their life. We are definitely the most comfortable generation ever on this planet. But in spite of that, can we say we are the most joyful? No. We are nowhere near that. So fixing the outside has not worked.

All of you are successful enough in your lives to understand that unless you do the right thing it does not work with the outside world. Have you come to this, or do you still believe that if your stars are okay, everything will work? Are you still in that condition where you believe you could do stupid things and with good stars everything will work well? Or do you understand that unless you do the right thing, it will not work with the outside reality?

The same is true with the interiority. Unless you do the right thing it will not work. Just because you are successful in the world – just because you were born into this family or that family– your happiness and your peace will not work unless you do the right thing internally. As it is true with the outside, it is true with the inside.

On a certain day, one man fell into a septic tank. I want you to imagine this – he fell into the septic tank, up to his neck in filth. He struggled to come out, but could not. Then after some amount of struggle, he started to scream, "Fire, fire, fire!" His neighbors heard the fire call and called the fire brigade. The firemen came and they looked around; there was no fire anywhere. Then they found this man in the septic tank, pulled him out and they asked, "Why are you screaming fire?" The man retorted, "If I said, shit, shit, would you have come?"

So you must do the right thing, otherwise it will not work. It does not matter how rich you get, how famous you get, how powerful you get, if you do not do the right thing internally, it will not work. Now what is the right thing to do internally? You think to be peaceful and happy are very fundamental aspirations of a human being, isn't it? Peace and happiness need not even be an aspiration in your life because you were born with them. To be peaceful and happy is square one of your life, yes? So it is not an aspiration. It is not an achievement in your life if you become peaceful, though these days even the so-called "spiritual" people are talking about this as if the highest goal in your life is peace of mind. You have no business to be any other way than peaceful.

Because everybody has gotten themselves so screwed up, now they are talking as if peace of mind is the biggest thing in their lives. If you want to enjoy your dinner today, you must be peaceful. Is enjoying your dinner today the biggest achievement in your life? Even your dog is doing it: you throw something to him, he enjoys eating it. But right now we think to be peaceful is a big achievement.

To be peaceful and happy are not the ultimate achievements of your life; they are the most fundamental requirements. Without them nothing tastes good in your life. Your food does not taste good, your husband, wife, children — nothing tastes good when you are not peaceful and happy. So being peaceful is not the ultimate. It is not something that you become. 'Rest in peace', you know? (*Laughs*) You started your life with peacefulness and happiness, isn't it?

So if this has to get somewhere, we need to understand the internal realities. Let us say you lost your peace today. What will happen? You go home and yell at your husband, or your wife, or whoever is there. If it continues, tomorrow morning you pick a quarrel with your neighbor. If it continues, tomorrow you go to your office and yell at your boss. The moment you yell at your boss, people know you need medical help. When you yelled at your wife, they thought it was normal. (*Laughs*) When you yell at your boss everybody knows you need medical help. So they take you to a doctor. Initially, the doctor tries to talk you out of it, but you will not budge. Then the next thing he does is put a pill into you.

One pill, and suddenly you feel very tranquil in your body and your mind – maybe just for a short period, but you do. It has worked, hasn't it? So what is a pill? Just a little bit of chemical. If you take the pill, you become peaceful. So if this little bit of chemical is creating peace in you, then definitely what you call peace is a certain type of chemistry, isn't it? What you call joy is another kind of chemistry. What you call anxiety, agony and ecstasy – each has a certain chemical basis to it.

Now I am talking about a whole science with which you create the right kind of chemistry. To be peaceful and joyful is just natural because that is how your chemistry is. You are no longer enslaved to external situations. No matter what is happening this is the way you are internally. And your body, your mind, your intelligence function at their best only when you are peaceful and happy, yes?

So whether you want to pursue your business, or your career, or your spirituality, or academics, or you just want to live with your family – it does not matter what you intend to pursue – every human being needs to do something about his interiority. If you do not do this, you live accidentally as a pain to yourself and to everybody around you. If you live accidentally, you do not decide how you should be. Right now, at this moment, if somebody else, or something else decides for you, you will be an extreme pain to yourself and to everybody else who is in touch with you. Lots of people have become like this. They are a pain unto themselves and to everybody else.

You may not be like this for twenty-four hours of the day, but I want you to understand, for you to break your life, you do not have to be insane for twenty-four hours of the day. If for five minutes a day you lose your temper, it is enough to break your life. If for five minutes a day you get angry with your wife or angry with your client – for only five minutes a day, not twenty-four hours – that is sufficient to ruin you. So what happens around you is something you cannot decide yourself one hundred percent. Only to some extent you can decide. At least what happens within you, you must decide.

See, there is nobody in the world that will be exactly the way you want them to be. Do you have at least one person in your life? No. There is no such possibility. Nobody will ever have such a person. It will not happen. If you think so, you are in a fool's paradise; life will knock you shortly.

At least *you* should happen the way you want to. You must definitely happen the way you want to. If this does not happen, then what is the point? Nothing will be worthwhile because everything becomes a struggle. Every simple act of life has become a struggle for people.

Right now, someone even mentioned that he is able to manage his stress better. See, why are you becoming stressed, first of all? A few years ago when I first came to the United States, wherever I went people were talking 'stress management', stress management'. I could not understand what was happening. Why would anybody want to manage his stress? I can understand you want to manage your business, your property, your family, your money, whatever else; but why would you want to manage your stress? You want to manage things that you value, is it not? Do you want to manage things that you do not care for? You want to manage things that you value in your life. I could not understand why anybody wanted to manage stress. It took me a while to understand, that people have come to the conclusion that there is no other way to live. They believe that stress is a part of life.

Stress is not a part of life. Stress is a part of life if you have lost your sanity, you understand? Stress is not happening because your job is difficult. Stress is happening because you are incapable of handling your own system. You do not know how to keep your body; you do not know how to keep your mind; you do not know how to keep your emotions; you do not know how to keep your energies. That is why you are stressed, not because of the job that you are doing. You ask an office boy, he says his job is stressful; you ask a President or a Prime Minister, he is also stressed; everybody else within that range is stressed. Then what other job is there in the world to do? No job in the world is stressful. You do not know how to keep your body, mind, emotions and energy, therefore, everything becomes stressful. If you know how to manage these, nothing is ever stressful.

"A thinking mind, a questioning mind, or a doubting mind cannot know faith. It is just a waste of time."

Questioner: Sadhguru, what is faith? Can you tell us something about faith?

Sadhguru: If faith was possible for you, it would be something that could propel you from one dimension to another without traversing the road. It is one big jump from here to there. But thinking minds, educated minds, questioning minds should never talk about faith because faith is not possible in a thinking mind. You need a very childlike mind, a very innocent mind, if you want to walk the path of faith. If you think and question logically, do not talk about faith; it will be fake.

Right now your faith is just about making deals with God, is it not? "Dear God, I will put ten thousand rupees in a temple or a church or a mosque, but I must get ten million in return." (*Laughs*) You try to make a deal like this with any person, and you say, "I will give you ten thousand rupees, and you give me ten million, this person will slap you and send you away." But you think the creator is such an idiot that he will make this kind of a deal with you. Can you just find one idiot in the whole city who will make this kind of a deal with you? No, but you think God is such an idiot. This is not faith, this is not devotion; this is deception.

If you want to walk the path of faith, you must be very childlike. If you want to walk the path of faith, it means that you have no agenda of your own for your life. You are willing to just go with whatever you are told. Today if your life has to go, you are not concerned, you just let it go – you must be like that. But you are not like that right now. For you, God has figured in your life only because somebody has told you he will fulfill your agenda. Let us be straight about it. You continuously go to one temple and when things do not work, if somebody tells you go to another one because better benefits will come, you will go there, won't you? You are constantly shifting from one temple to another, are you not?

So as far as you are concerned, your idea of God is like this: if you pay hundred rupees in any shop you will get only hundred rupees of goods, but if you pay hundred rupees to God, you will get thousand rupees worth of goods. This is the general idea.

If you look at all the prayers in the world, ninety-nine percent of the prayers are always about, "Dear God, give me this, give me that, protect me, save me." Fundamentally, your prayer is coming either out of greed or out of fear. Does this look like divinity to you or does it look like survival to you? It is simple, basic survival. It is just that every creature on the planet — from a worm to an insect, an animal to a bird — handles its own survival. But human beings, who claim to be the most intelligent of all the species, route their survival through heaven. And it has not worked.

If you want to survive well on this planet, you just have to learn to use these four limbs and your few brain cells properly. Only those people who learn to use their body and mind properly will survive well on this planet. People who are looking up and praying are constantly in a pit.

India as a nation is a clear example of that. We have three hundred thousand gods in this country, but still half the people cannot even eat properly. Survival has not been taken care of by all these gods, because gods cannot take care of it. If you want to survive well, you just have to learn to use your body and mind properly. There is no other way to survive. It is just that it gives you some confidence to say, "God is with me." Okay, if it is a psychological ploy, use it. I am not against it, but now you are not talking faith. That is different. Faith means you have no agenda in life. You are willing to go with God's agenda.

Many people have spoken about faith, but you know Jesus said, "Only children will know the kingdom of God." When he said that, he was not talking about little children. He meant only those who are childlike can know the path of faith. Faith is possible only if you are very innocent of mind. A thinking mind, a questioning mind, a doubting mind cannot know faith. It will be just a waste of time.

The reason why faith has been promoted so much worldwide is because it is an ancient phenomenon. Another aspect of it is, even now within you, if you look at your body, your mind, your emotions and your energy, you know maximum intensity only in your emotions, is it not? Most people do not know what it means to have an intense body; most people do not know their bodies are sedate. Most people do not know what it means to have an intense mind. Energies are intense only for a very few people. But emotions can get intense. Very easily your emotions can gain intensity. So it is because of this that so much has been said about faith in the world; it is easier to get your emotions to peak intensity. To get your body there, to get your mind there, to get your energies there, it would take a different level of understanding and work. But with emotions, everybody can get intense.

So what was generally taught was about getting people's emotions intense. But today with modern education and your exposure to other things, your emotions are not the most dominant factor of your life in twenty-four hours. Your mind has become the dominant factor. Once your mind is the dominant factor, you cannot walk the path of faith. It is not possible. Just for convenience and comfort, you believe in something.

Please look at your life: you see that you are keeping God on the side only as insurance. Everything that is vital to your life, you keep in your hands. But you keep God on the side because you say, "I have also paid the premium in case something goes wrong." If you have so much faith, why do you not put all your valuables and all the money you have on the street and say, "Dear God, do what you want. What is mine you give me; what is not mine, you let it go." Are you able to do that? No. Whatever is important to you, you keep in your hands. So God has become just an insurance policy. In this way, faith will not work.

People who walk the path of faith are insane people as far as society is concerned. The Mirabais and the Ramakrishna Paramahamsas of the world are people who are absolutely insane people, as far as society is concerned. Today after a thousand years you worship them; that is easy. When they lived, people thought they were utterly crazy. Yes or no? Let us say your neighbor in the middle of the night jumps into your garden, hugs your tree and cries loudly. Would you think he was enlightened? Or would you think he was drunk or plain crazy? If you had Ramakrishna as your neighbor, this is how the situation would be. Or in your house, your wife thinks she is married to a god. Would you think she has reached divinity, or would you think she needs psychiatric treatment? This is living with Mirabai.

You need to understand that people who walked the path of faith were in ecstasy, in a fantastic place within themselves, but as far as the social situation was concerned, they were always a problem. You have no intention to walk the path of faith so intensely that you do not care what happens to your life in the society around you. So when you are not like that, you should not talk about faith. You had better learn to use your body, your mind, and your energies properly; because through every one of these there is a way.

If you use your emotions and try to reach your ultimate nature, we call this bhakti yoga. If you use your intelligence and try to reach your ultimate nature, we call this gnana yoga. If you try to use your physical body, or action, and try to reach your ultimate nature, we call this karma yoga. If you use your inner energies to transform them and reach your ultimate nature, we call this kriya yoga. So one is the yoga of devotion, another is the yoga of intelligence, another is the yoga of action, and the fourth is the yoga of transforming energies.

Now, what this fundamentally means is that you must use your head, heart, hands, and energy properly. Is there anybody here who is only one big head, with no heart, no hands, and no energy? Or one big heart, and not the other three? You are a combination of these four things. Each individual here is a unique combination of the same four things. So, you need a combination of all these four. You need to handle all of them together; only then you will progress.

It is like driving a car. You must take all the four wheels where you want to go. If you try to take just one wheel there, your car is going to become a big struggle. If these four wheels try to travel in four different directions, you are going to have lots of trouble with your vehicle. So if you align these four wheels in one direction, then the car flows in harmony. You have to employ all the four dimensions. The reason why in the tradition so much stress has always been laid on the presence of a living master is only because he will mix these four dimensions in a proper concoction for you. If I give the yoga that I give to this person, to another person, it will not work. He needs a unique kind of combination, because he is a unique combination of these four dimensions. It needs the right mixture; only then it works.

So just having faith does not work. If you go on an exclusive path like that then you will see you get completely dislocated from the social situations in which you exist. Bhaktas are not people whom you can live with because they do not care for anything. They just do not care for anything around them, except their object of devotion. That is how they will be; they are very wonderful people within themselves, but socially they are not regarded as good people.

—⊱⋆⊰—

"Your mind is like a tape recorder...It is always listening to you and it is very faithfully recording everything... Now the problem is that ...at the wrong time it plays the wrong music."

Questioner: How do you make your mind listen to you?

Sadhguru: (*Laughs*) The mind need not listen to you. What you call 'my mind' is actually just society's garbage bin. Your mind is like a basket; wherever you go, in society you gather and gather all sorts of things in the basket. That is your mind. What kind of mind you have right now — if you look at it carefully — is very much the kind of mind which has known a certain type of exposure. If you were born in a remote part of Africa, for example, you would be thinking and feeling completely differently.

So, what your mind is — or right now the content of your mind— is just the data that you have fed into it. It is your exposure to life. It is just that most of it went in unconsciously. A little bit of it went in consciously, but most of it went into your mind unconsciously.

What you call 'my mind' right now is a complex amalgam of all the impressions that you have taken through the five sense organs every moment of your life. Everything that you see, everything that you hear, everything that you smell, taste and touch, goes into your mind and becomes a certain kind of content. Depending upon what type of input went in, your mind developed certain tendencies accordingly. So, you consider a certain tendency, a certain inclination as your personality. It is just a complex mess of things which have gathered unconsciously. It could have also been gathered consciously. But right now it has been gathered unconsciously.

So, the mind need not listen to you. The mind is just a bank of information. If you are conscious, you would use it to the extent that is necessary. You would use it to your benefit. If you are unconscious, you are using it to your detriment. Anything in the world (it does not matter if it is beautiful or ugly), if you know about it, if you know how to use it, can be useful. Even the filthiest aspects in the world, if you know clearly what is what, the knowledge could enhance your life, if you are consciously using it. If you are unconscious, then everything can be a detriment to your life.

Your mind is like a tape recorder which has just recorded everything. It was kept on, whether you were awake or asleep. This tape recorder was constantly kept on, and it just recorded and recorded. It is always listening to you and it is very faithfully recording everything. Now the problem is that it is also playing without your permission what it has already recorded. (*Laughs*) It is simply playing whatever you recorded, whether you like it or not. At the wrong time it plays the wrong music. That is the thing.

You have this much control over your body: if you want your hand here, it goes here; you want it there, it goes there. Please try this with your mind: you want to put your mind here, it goes there; you want to put it there, it goes somewhere else. Now, with this kind of mind, where are you trying to go, anyway? If you have gotten somewhere in your life, it must have happened by accident. Suppose you want your car to go here and it goes there. Is it safe to be in this automobile? Only if it is going where you want it to go is it worth getting into this vehicle. Otherwise, this is a dangerous vehicle. You get into your automobile only for a few hours a day. But it is through the vehicle of your mind that you travel the whole of your life. Suppose you are using an out-of-control vehicle, and you expect to reach somewhere, it is not going to work.

Suppose you are driving your car and it went out of control. What is the first thing you would like to do?

Questioner: Jump out.

Sadhguru: You want to jump out? It is not an airplane!

It does not matter how; your only concern is that you want somehow to stop it. When your car goes out of control, the only thing you want to do is to stop it. Right now that is exactly what you need to do with your mind. If you can consciously still your mind, even for a few moments a day, suddenly you will find your mind will become a miracle.

This mind is a miracle, and right now it is being used in a disastrous way. This mind could have produced ecstasy for you. It could have been a ladder to the divine, but right now it has become a source of misery. Where is all the human misery in this world being manufactured? Where is the manufacturing unit? It is the mind. Just think, what should have been a miracle has become a misery, not because there is anything wrong with your mind, but simply because you are operating it unconsciously.

So, your mind is just a complex accumulation of information. If you were conscious, you would know what to take in, what not to take in. Now you are unconscious, so it looks like it is throwing everything at you. It is not throwing everything; it is just a garbage bin. Whatever the topmost layer of garbage is today, that would determine the kind of smell that is coming out. That is all your mind is.

You have heard of a word called Buddha? Probably if I say Buddha, you generally think in terms of Gautama the Buddha. Gautama is not the only Buddha. Buddha is not his second name. He became a Buddha. There have been thousands of Buddhas, and there still are. 'Bu' means 'buddhi' or the 'intellect'. 'Dha' means 'one who is above'. One who is above his intellect is a Buddha. One who is into his intellect is a nonstop suffering human being; that is where you are right now.

Right now, you may think you are not suffering. Please see, your misery is right behind you. Right now situations are okay. If you turn back and see, your misery is right there. You are watching the morning sunrise and everything is fantastic. But if you turn back and see, your anxiety and your pain and your suffering will be right behind you all the time. Because once you are into the intellect, your misery is inevitable. This is the way it works. If you rise above this, you are completely free of it.

If you are below it, you also do not know so much suffering. Animals do not know the kind of suffering that human beings know. With their stomach full, animals are quite fine. Do you see this? With you, it is not like that. If your stomach is empty, you have only one problem: you need food. With your stomach full, you have one hundred problems. Because your problem is not coming from the outside; your problem is coming from the inside. Endlessly it is being manufactured. If you solve one problem, you see ten waiting in queue. Because it is not by solving problems that you get there. There is only one problem, and that is you. If you dissolve this one problem, only then there will be no other problem.

Now, if you create the necessary awareness where you are above the basic function of the mind, if you are a witness to your own mind, and if you are above the process of the mind, there is no such thing as suffering, because all suffering is of the mind. Once you are out of the mind, there can be no suffering. I know if somebody tells you that you are out of your mind, you will get insulted. Do not. If somebody says you are out of your mind, they are paying you the highest compliment. They are telling you, you are a Buddha, you know? The misunderstanding is you think being out of your mind means madness. Madness is always of the mind. If you are out of the mind, how can you be mad? You will be perfectly sane, absolutely sane.

Do you call a person who is causing misery to himself, a sane person or an insane person? A mind which could cause joy, which could cause ecstasy, is right now causing misery. That means knowingly or unknowingly you are causing misery to yourself. So anybody who causes misery to himself is definitely not in a right state of existence. You may say, "No, no, do you know what happened in my life?" It does not matter what happened in your life. Your misery does not come because of something that happened in your life. Your misery is there because you have no say in what your mind does. It is doing its own nonsense; that is why you are miserable.

Right now, you are wrongly identified with many things that you are not, so the mind is just running crazy. Once you are identified with things that you are not, you try to hold your mind; it is not going to work. You try as hard as you can; it is not going to work. There is no other way. If you dis-identify yourself with everything that you are not, then you will see the mind is simply a blank space. If you want, you can turn it on, otherwise it is off.

If I lock myself up for five or six days, I do not have a single thought in my mind for those five or six days. I do not think, I do not write, I do not read, I do not do anything; I am just being alive. Being alive is a sufficient phenomenon; it is a tremendous phenomenon by itself. It is not that you have to think and make it beautiful, no. Life is happening right now. This is the biggest phenomenon.

But right now, you are not enjoying the creation the way it

is. You've got your own petty creation in your head. You are busy with that. Ninety percent of the time you are only thinking about life, not living life. And what nonsense can you think about life? Life can only be experienced. What you think is all coming from the data that you have already gathered. Whatever data, no matter how much you have gathered, is still a very limited possibility. From that limited possibility you go on thinking, thinking, and thinking...

It is not by thinking that you know life. It is by the clarity of your vision that you know life. This will happen to you only if you are not identified with anything. Only then can you have involvement with everything, without entanglement. You are deeply involved with life, but you do not know any entanglement because you are not identified with anything. Now you see that your mind can be turned on if you want; otherwise, it is off. That is how it should be.

You are sitting here right now. If your body starts doing its own thing without your permission, would not it be very ridiculous? Yes? Right now your mind is doing that all the time and it is very ridiculous. Your only comfort is that you think other people are not able to see it (*Laughs*) but other people can see it. You think it is not seen? It is seen.

Different people are using it in different ways, in different capacities, and in different possibilities. It once happened that an American tourist was driving through Egypt and his car broke down in a remote place. He thought he was lost. Then a villager came on a bullock cart, and with sign language he requested help. The villager said, "Okay." He tied the car to the bullock cart and towed it to the nearest town. They got the car fixed; the American was happy, and he went away.

He wanted to somehow reward the villager who helped him out of the difficult situation. So he decided to give him a gift; and the gift was an airplane. He bought a small airplane that was delivered to the village. The villager looked at the airplane; up and down he looked at the plane, and thought, "Okay, he has given me a high-tech bullock cart." He yoked his bulls to the airplane, and sat in the airplane. The bulls went about drawing the airplane around; he was happy and the people were all looking up to him. The thought he had got such a wonderful bullock cart.

One day, by accident, he touched the starter button and the engine roared. Then he thought, "Oh, the American has sent me a different shaped car than the one that he was driving." So now the villager started driving it around in the village. People were amazed that this guy had a car. One day, just by chance, he moved the joystick, and the plane flew. Only then he finally knew he had got an airplane.

Your mind is like that; it can be used on many different levels. It can be used to such a peak that it can become the source of you, and the source of great ecstasy within you. Or you can use it to do mundane things. Or you can use it to create misery for yourself. It is up to you. How would you use anything? Whether it is for your well-being or for your detriment just depends on how conscious you are at that moment. If you were consciously living your life, would you cause misery to yourself? Never.

When you exist unconsciously, large parts of you are still unconscious, so misery is possible. Because misery is possible you ask this question, "When will my mind listen to me?" Your mind should tell you things that you could not imagine. Why should it listen to you? Because it is causing misery right now. It has become burdensome, so the question comes up. This is because large parts of you are still unconscious. The problem arises not because of the mind, not because of the body, but because we are handling and driving both of them unconsciously. When you drive something unconsciously, everything becomes a problem in your life.

"If you are truly intelligent, you should not be doing what people expect; you should be just doing what is best for yourself and everybody around you even if it is at the cost of being unpopular."

Questioner: How do we handle the pressure of expectations in daily life?

Sadhguru: Whose expectations, yours or others?

Questioner: Mine

Sadhguru: What are your expectations? Your expectations

are not about you; your expectations are all socially conditioned. Have you noticed how your expectations keep changing constantly every year or even faster these days? (*Laughs*) So if your expectations are constantly changing, it means you do not even know what you want. When you do not know what you want, what you ask for should not happen, should it? If you know what you want, what you ask for should happen to you. When you do not know what you want, if what you ask for does not happen, you are better off.

Your expectations are simply and generally a reaction to the social situations in which you live. You expect to become this way or that way because somebody else has become this way or that way. More than that, other people have expectations of you. Not only do you have expectations about your life, but other people have them too. They have investments in you too. You have to bear the necessary profit for them; otherwise they will not keep quiet. (*Laughs*) They have made their investments, and they want their dividend. If it does not come, they will bother you in so many ways.

So, these expectations — what is expected of that person or this person, or yourself — are all things that come from a social arrangement. You have to fulfill them to some extent, but that shouldn't become the basis of directing your life. If you go by people's expectations, you will find that people's expectations are always concerned with what is already there. If you are truly intelligent, you should not be doing what people expect. You should be just doing what is best for yourself and everybody around you; even if it is at the cost of being unpopular. It is okay.

—◦◦◦◦—

"There is sufficient unpleasantness in the world. Where is the need for you to make yourself unpleasant?"

Questioner: How does one conquer one's negativity and anger? Is it possible?

Sadhguru: Why do you want to conquer them? See, you want to conquer something that you value. Do you want to conquer something that you do not value? Why would you take the trouble of conquering something that is of no value to you? Would you want to go and conquer a wasteland? Or would you rather go and conquer a rich land? If you are a king, what would you want to conquer? You would like to conquer a rich kingdom, not a wasteland. You do not want to go and conquer a desert. So why do you want to conquer something you do not want?

Questioner: Because we like to control.

Sadhguru: I know, I understand. (*Laughs*) So first drop the idea of conquering. Right now, are you angry? No. So why should you conquer anger? It does not even exist. How do you control or conquer that which does not exist? Once in a while you get angry. Why do you get angry? Because suddenly your body, your mind, your energies are not behaving the way you want them to. They are just doing their own nonsense suddenly. That is anger. So, anger is not in constant existence. Trying to control or conquer that which is not in existence is just going to be a wasteful effort.

Sometimes your mind turns unpleasant. Or in other words, sometimes you turn unpleasant. One form of your unpleasantness is referred to as anger. Other forms of unpleasantness are called by many other names. We will just take anger as an example. Why would anybody make himself unpleasant? There is sufficient unpleasantness in the world. Where is the need for you to make yourself unpleasant?

Right now you are in this kind of childish behavior that if situations around you are unpleasant, you will also become unpleasant. Tell me, is there any intelligence in this? Especially if the situations around you are unpleasant, is it not all the more important that you be very pleasant within yourself? But right now you are in this childish mode that if outside situations turn unpleasant, you will make your inside also terribly unpleasant. There is no intelligence in this.

Somewhere when it comes to ourselves, we refuse to employ our intelligence. I am not telling you, do not get angry. It is up to you. If it is a pleasant experience, get angry all the time; but generally whenever you get angry, you suffer more than your victim, yes? What is the point? Why would you create unpleasantness to yourself? There is enough unpleasantness in the world however or wherever you walk in the world, you will step into something unpleasant here or there. However you try to avoid it, somewhere you will step into some unpleasantness. Is it a necessity that you have to manufacture your own private unpleasantness? No. So why are you creating things that you do not want? You just do not know what you are doing with yourself; that is the only reason.

Try to do one thing with your eyes closed; try to drive home with your eyes closed. You may make it one day, you know. You may bump off a few people and still make it home. But try for a few days, and you will not live more than two days. So right now it is just like that. You are trying to handle your well-being with your eyes closed. You will not know well-being, no matter what you do. You have to handle it with your eyes open.

"People think by knowing other people they can become effective… but it is not true. If you know yourself, you can become very effective in the world."

Questioner: Sadhguru, sometimes in my life I feel I can read a bit into people's minds, and sometimes I feel it is just my ego judging them. How can I know the difference between the two? And even when I do, should I act upon that or just take people at face value?

Sadhguru: You are able to read people's minds – is this what you are saying?

There is a very deep misunderstanding in the world about being effective. People think by knowing other people they can be very effective. The idea is, if I know you, I can make this situation go my way. This is the idea, but it is not true. If you know yourself, you can become very effective in the world. If you do not make any attempts to read something or perceive something or judge something, but simply learn to look at everything the way it is, you will see things the way they are. But if you make an effort to read – and sometimes you will, because, after all, you have a mind – you may read certain things. That's because you have perception, and you can judge. But what will you do with these judgments?

See, today the whole modern world is just about this. For example, everything about science today is about how to make use of everything for our well-being. Whatever we see, we want to see how we can use it. We see this tree, we see this rock, we see this water, and we want to see how to use them all. We cannot just see anything simply the way it is and leave it there. This goes not just for nature; this goes for people, also.

Once you get into this mindset, whoever you see, you say, "Okay, how can I make use of these people?" This is a serious misunderstanding that has happened in the world. It has sunk so deep into humanity that today people are being used, and things are being loved. You have seen couples divorce each other; have you seen anybody divorcing their money? No.

Questioner: It is impossible.

Sadhguru: When you are in a certain misunderstanding of life, it is impossible. So, we are using people and loving things. But if people are here to be loved, where is the need to read them? There is no need to read them.

Now, probably when you come to a yoga program, you saw a certain form of greeting; unknowingly many of you are beginning to do the 'namaste' gesture. Usually, when you see a person, it is their body that you see. If you look at this person's body, immediately your mind will say, "Oh, she is beautiful," or "she is ugly", or "she is young", or "she is old". All these things will happen in the mind in a split second. If you try to judge her behavior, or speech, or something else, then all kinds of judgments will happen. You may like her, or dislike her; you may hate her, or love her; all these thoughts may come to your mind.

However, with the namaste greeting you do not look at her body, or her mind, or at her emotions; you address the deepest core in this person, to start with. First, you bow down to the seed of life which exists in this being. Whatever is the source of all life around us is what you refer to as God, is it not?

Questioner: Yes.

Sadhguru: Does that source of life that seed of life exist in the lady you greet, or in whoever stands in front of you? Now with the namaste you have bowed down to that source of life as your first involvement. Afterwards you meet the other things in the person. The body may be okay or not okay, but you have no issues about that. The mind may be okay or not okay, but you have no problem with that. This person may agree with your culture or may not; it is okay. Whether you like that person or not, it does not matter because with the namaste, you have first addressed the fundamental source of life.

So this is not a judgment, nor is it a reading. If you go about trying to read people, invariably it is a judgment, isn't it? And a human being is not a constant factor. This person may be one way today; tomorrow morning she maybe another way. Today she may be something that you do not like. Tomorrow morning she may be in a wonderful mood. But if you think you have read and made an impression of that person in the past, then you will miss that person the way she is right now.

You know the first parable about Adam and Eve? God told them to eat whatever they wanted except from a particular tree — the Tree of knowledge. Knowledge means your impression of things, your reading of the world, not the way the world is. Knowledge means the impressions that you have taken in. The more knowledge you have, the less you experience. So when it comes to life, do not gather knowledge; experience it the way it is right now. If you come here in winter, the trees will all be dry sticks. You do not make a judgment about these trees when you look at them in the winter. Nor do you make a judgment about them when you look at them in spring.

So similarly human beings, many times during one day, go

through winters, summers and springs. Not everybody is able to maintain a constant spring within himself. In India, we call spring 'vasant' or 'basant'. People are named like this. Basanti means that this woman is spring, always in full bloom. Life is going on in full intensity. But not everybody is like that. Sometimes they are spring; sometimes they become winter; and sometimes so many other things.

So do not get into that; because once you get into that, it is an endless trap. Even if the mind makes judgments about other people, do not attach any importance to them. Because once you start making judgments, you realize there are only two basic judgments: good or bad. There may be many colors to it, but fundamentally, there are only two judgments, is it not? Something is good, or something is bad. You are naturally drawn to, and get attached to, what you consider to be good. Everything that you consider bad, you repel, and negative emotions flow.

Once you get attached to something, once your intellect gets attached to something, it gets distorted. It cannot see anything the way it is. See, right now, you are looking at me; where do you see me? I am not here. As far as you are concerned, I am within you. You are not seeing me here; light is falling upon me, reflecting my image, going through your lenses, then falling on your cornea, getting inverted, and then getting corrected in the screen of your mind, isn't it? If this screen of your mind is like a plain mirror, you will see things clearly. Suppose the mirror became wonky, do you know what kind of images you would see? Once your mind gets identified with something, you do not have a plain mirror. You have a distorted mirror. Whatever you see in it will be a completely wrong impression of everything.

So, the most important thing that a human being needs to do is to keep his intellect free of all identifications. One should not get identified, even with fundamental things, such as a man or as a woman, this or that. You are identified with your body, with your family, with your education, with your religion, with your nationality, with your race, with a million other things.

The intellect should be kept free from this identification; that is when your intellect is like a sharp knife that cuts through everything and shows everything the way it is. Otherwise, everything gets distorted. Once you get into this judgmental thing, all kinds of things will stick to this knife. Once too many things stick to the knife, this knife loses its penetration. It cannot show you life the way it is. So do not get into those judgments. There is no need to judge. You just have to judge situations. You do not have to judge people.

"The mind is physical; it is subtle, very subtle, but still it is physical."

Questioner: You say our mind is just an accumulation of various impressions, and the body is also gathered from outside. So is this whole life process just a kind of recycling?

Sadhguru: Recycling? Yes, in a way the physical is always being recycled. You know the countless number of people who lived on this planet before you and I came here — all those millions and millions of people that must have walked this planet before we came here, where are they right now? They became top soil, and they became vegetables, and we ate them up. Or you allowed further recycling, you allowed the goats to eat the vegetables, and then you ate the goats. Or you directly ate them, whichever way.

So, the physical body is being recycled. Are you not? You are constantly being recycled even today. Now is the mind being recycled? Have not all the people in your life — your parents, your teachers, your preachers — put a lot of nonsense into your head? Have they not passed on to you whatever they picked up from somewhere else? Are you not trying to put it into your children? So the recycling of the mind is also happening. I wish at least the mind was fresh, but the old nonsense is being recycled. Now you are talking about the very life process itself; is it a recycle?

See, when you talk about the physical, you mean the body and the mind. The body is physical; very clearly you can understand that. The mind is also physical, just like this light bulb. It is very clearly visible that it is physical, but the electricity behind it is also physical, yes? And the light that it emits is also physical. Right now whether it is this light or the sunlight (the biggest source of light that we know), if I want, I can just stop it with my hand and leave a shadow of darkness. Because it is physical, I can stop it. If it was not physical this hand could not be raised to stop the light.

So it is the same with the mind; the mind is also physical. If I want, I can throw this pen at you. Similarly if I want, I can throw a thought at you. The mind is physical; subtle, very subtle, but still physical. It belongs to the physical realm. When we talk about the physical, your understanding and logic is in a certain way.

So the dimensions of the physical need to be looked at logically because they are within the limitations of logic; when you say physical, there is this and that. Only if there are two, there is logic. You need a minimum of two to do anything logical, isn't it? If there is only one, then there is no logic.

Logic means there are two polarities, two opposites. Because there is you and me, there is logic. If there is only me, there is no logic; there is no need for it. It cannot exist. If there is only you, there is no logic; similarly, if only me, there is no logic. When you and I are there, there is logic.

The physical always exists within a limited boundary. The physical can be small, or it can be big, but never without a boundary. The physical always has boundaries. Once there is a boundary, there is something within the boundary, and something outside the boundary. So the physical demands logic. If you handle the physical without logic, you will be a fool. But if you try to handle life itself logically, once again you will be a fool. Do you understand?

Why people go on struggling is because they logically make some things work in their life. Because it worked well, they try to extend this logic to every aspect of their life, and they just mess themselves up completely. Somebody else operates some other part of life illogically and it works well. They try to extend this to all aspects of life, and again it becomes a mess. They do not understand that the physical needs logic. For that which is beyond the physical, logic is useless.

See, the materialistic people have employed logic and created comfort and physical well-being for themselves. Because they have been successful with that, they try hard to experience the beyond also logically. It will not work. The so-called spiritual people have certain things working illogically. Because of that they extended the illogic to everyday life and became absolutely ridiculous. Do you not see this happening all the time? They talk utter nonsense about life because they experience a certain part of life which is illogical. It worked very well there; and now they are trying to extend that to the simple mundane aspects of life. No. The mundane, the physical, has to be handled logically, but what is beyond has to be handled illogically.

Now, in a way, recycling means coming and going. When you are talking about a dimension beyond the physical, there is no coming, there is no going. Only the physical can come, and only the physical can go. The physical can rise, and the physical can fall; that which is beyond the physical, neither rises nor falls; it neither comes nor goes. If you try to explain it logically, you will only make a fool of yourself.

⟶⟐⟵

"The mind is incapable of being aware. It is only because of the mind that you have become unaware."

Questioner: What is the difference between mental awareness and mental sharpness? You've often talked of the difference, but I don't think I understand.

Sadhguru: The mind is incapable of being aware. It is only because of the mind that you have become unaware. It is only the activity of the mind which has brought unawareness into you. So the question of mind and awareness together does not arise.

The moment your experience of life is beyond the limitations of the mind is when you are really aware. The mind is capable of being sharp. It had better be; otherwise, you will even miss the jokes. (*Laughs*) When you miss the joke, you become the joke. Is it not so? Let that not happen to you. So the mind should be sharpened, but the problem with you is that the moment you have a sharp mind, you become terribly identified with it.

See, if you have a no-good body, you would think of bodilessness. (*Laughs*) Now when you have a good body, or at least the kind of body which draws people's attention, you do not think of bodilessness; you think only body, is it not? See, that is what has happened to whole cultures of people. As people attach more and more importance to the body, everything about them becomes the body.

Right now, on a large scale, it has happened in Western societies. The body has become the most important aspect of people's lives. Now, just look at the promotional aspect. If you look at the advertising in a society, you understand what attracts people and what the prime concern is in people's minds, because advertising is about selling. If something has to be sold, it has to appeal to you. You take something as subtle as fragrance; fragrance is a subtle thing, but fragrance is all about sex, is it not? The kind of smells that we are talking about, and the kind of fragrance that is being advertised, is all about inducing sex, or exciting sexuality, isn't it?

So fragrance has become a huge tool to enhance bodily pleasure. If you look at the Eastern cultures, fragrance is an important part of the spiritual process. In any temple, in any prayer house, in any pooja room, in any little shrine, there is a certain kind of fragrance. This is not at all about the body. Just the simple aspect of using smells, if you look at it culturally, is oriented either towards the body or beyond the body.

The same is true of everything else. Take music, for example. Today modern music is performed on stage by a man and a woman who do everything they can do but in vertical postures – with clothes on, of course. Is it not so? It is no more about music; it is all about the physical body. If you can sing well, you are no more a musician; you must be able to gyrate. So the major trend – and I am just using this as an example, and I am not branding anybody as anything – has also become a tool towards bodily pleasure. But at the same time, classical music has always been about going beyond physical limitations.

Traditionally, people talk about God and the devil as two opposites. You must understand, once you put God and the devil as opposites, they become equals in their own right, and in their own spheres of life. They become equals; and that is why most of the time the devil wins. So what is being referred to as God and the devil is just this: what is physical is considered the devil; what is beyond the physical is considered God.

Now, once you understand it this way, your very longing or your mental understanding will always be "Okay, how do we kill the physical? We want to kill the devil." You cannot kill the physical. If you try to kill the physical, you will obliterate yourself in some way. You will become crippled, damaged, distorted. You will not become free; you will not become liberated. So the very basis of understanding that one is against the other creates a huge problem in the mind. Once you understand that this is opposite to that, and that is opposite to this, then whichever you seek, one will destroy the other. And once you do not accept one half of existence, the question of you knowing anything of the beyond does not arise.

I mentioned some time ago that rithambhara means 'that which is the very source of the cosmos', and ritha means 'the foundation of the cosmos'. So 'that which is the foundation of the cosmos' includes both good and bad, or it has no distinction between good and bad. It just sees creation as creation. It does not see anything as ugly or beautiful; it does not see anything as good or bad; it does not see anything as God or devil. It just sees everything the way it is. That is awareness.

The mind can only function with discretion; otherwise the mind is useless. The mind as a faculty is useful to you only because it can discriminate between what is good and what is bad, what is right and what is wrong, isn't it?

If you move into your awareness, you explode into the oneness of existence. If you move into the mind, you move into the discretion of splitting the world into pieces. So these two things are completely different. Ignorant people are always talking about awareness of the mind. There is no such thing. But for ages ignorance has ruled the planet, and it continues to rule. The major forces in the planet have always been of ignorance, not of awareness.

What I am telling you is, you must be clear about what you are seeking. Right now when you are not clear about what you are seeking, you will always be going one step forward, one step backward. Someone who takes one step forward then one step backward obviously will not go anywhere. If you walk forward, it is beautiful; if you walk backwards, at least you realize where you are going. But if you are one step forward, one step backward, you will remain in confusion for the whole of your life. You will remain in frustration for your whole life.

So if you are planning to walk backwards, you are in the

wrong place. If you are planning to take one step forward, one step backward, it is tragic that you have to be here. If you are planning to walk forward, you must be clear where you are going, and what it is that you are seeking.

Once it happened. Two priests were standing with a signboard in their hands which read, 'The end is near; turn yourself around before it is too late.' One speeding car came along; the driver saw the sign, put his head out of the window, and said, "Leave us alone, you religious nuts," and he sped on. He went beyond the corner. Then the priests heard the screeching of tires and a huge crash. Then one of the priests said to the other, "Maybe we just have the signboard read: 'Bridge is out'."

Wrong signs have been shown to you for a very long time. So do not mix up the mind and awareness. You cannot cultivate awareness; you can cultivate the mind. You can do many things with the mind. But you cannot do anything with awareness, because what you refer to as awareness is the very basis of who you are. Right now you can say "I am here" only because there is some sense of awareness, is it not? Though awareness is struggling to penetrate itself through the mass of your mind, it has still managed to find some expression. That is awareness, but it is right now struggling its way through the mass of your mind.

If you keep the mind aside, awareness will blossom in a huge way. It has already blossomed; the whole existence is just that, but now it will come into your experience.

—◦◦◦◦—

"The whole existence is just one energy manifesting itself in a million different ways."

Questioner: My question is about energy. Can one kind of energy dominate another? Whatever the energy is, human or inhuman, good or bad, in whatever condition or time, can it dominate another energy?

Sadhguru: You have heard of Albert Einstein, haven't you? You know he gave you one famous formula, $E = mc2$. What this means on one level is that the whole existence is just one energy manifesting itself in a million different ways. Or in other words, what he is saying is the water that is falling is energy. That same energy is standing here as a tree. That same energy is sitting here as you. That same energy is sitting here as me. That same energy is standing up as a rock. This is what Einstein was trying to prove.

Is he correct? He is correct, no question about it. Is he right? No. Do you understand the difference? He is mathematically correct. But is his perception completely right? No. He is correct. He has not made a mistake; he is definitely correct — the same realities have been expressed in so many different ways.

Modern science proves to you beyond any doubt now that everything is the same energy. The religions of the world for ages have been screaming, "God is everywhere." Whether you say God is everywhere, or everything is the same energy, it is the same reality expressed in two different ways.

Scientists have mathematically deduced it. Religious people have just come to believe it. But for both of them it is not a living reality yet. Because of this, life does not change. By discovering this, Einstein's life did not change in any fundamental way. The lives of millions of people who believe this have not changed either because it has not become a living reality.

Now you ask this question, "Can one energy dominate another energy?" There is only one energy. How can it dominate the other? But does it mean to say that all these people do not exist as different people? They do, do they not?

Now if you take this person as one kind of energy, and that person as another, can this energy dominate that one? It definitely can. But now it would be improper to call this 'this energy dominating that one'. This person can dominate that person; physically, mentally, emotionally, energy-wise too. But it is not 'this energy' versus 'that energy'; it is 'this person versus that person', or one person using his energy to dominate another. Is it possible? Definitely. It is definitely possible.

Now when water is falling over a period of time and wearing out the rocks, it becomes dominating energy in some way. Similarly, with human beings, they can also dominate by using their energies in a particular way.

If you are asking in terms of occult, or in terms of certain arts and sciences, can people try to dominate somebody else's life, or somebody else's course of life itself? It is possible, but to a large extent it is psychological, because the most dominant emotion in most people on this planet is fear. Because of this, almost everything that they do in their lives is in search of security. Fear is always in the background; it is all the time there. It is sometimes above the surface, sometimes below the surface, but it is there all the time. So because of this if you just put an idea into somebody's mind that "you are being used," or "you are being dominated," that is enough.

See, I do not have to do any real voodoo stuff to you. Tomorrow morning when you come out of the house, let us say we opened up the stomach of your pet cat, put the intestines out, hung him in front of your house, and we made some signs and marks, and chanted some strange stuff, what would you do? I know no voodoo – I just arranged a little bit of blood and gore in front of your house. When you come out and see this, you would get very terrified. Then I make a phone call and say, "You have just had a glimpse of what will happen today." You will do all kinds of disastrous things to yourself in the next twenty-four hours because the nature of the mind is like that.

There are very few people who can just dismiss the nonsense and go on with what they are doing; very few. All others, their mind will function in such ways that they will trip upon themselves and fall. They do not need any outside energies to dominate them. Because their mind is so un-established, with a little bit of manipulation you can easily get them churning in whichever direction you want. That is also one kind of dominance. But if you are asking if there is such a thing as energy dominance, definitely there is.

There is a whole science and art in that direction. Have you heard of the Vedas? They are the oldest scriptures on the planet. We say they are over a hundred thousand years old. So among the Vedas, the last one is called the Atharva Veda. This is all about how to use energies to your benefit, and somebody else's detriment. But people who walk the spiritual path should never look that way, because it is an entanglement. It does not enhance your life. It gets you entangled in so many deep ways.

<hr />

"Desire is a natural longing. Love is an emotional expression of that desire."

Questioner: Is there a natural longing for love in every human being? And is it related in some way to the energy that is common in everything around us?

Sadhguru: See, love is an emotion. What is this emotion about? If you look at what you call 'love' – on the emotional plane – you find it is a longing in you to become one with something, or somebody. Emotionally, you are trying to make what is two into one. Making everything into one is called yoga. In a way, you are trying yoga in a small way. You are trying yoga in a uni-dimensional way. You are trying yoga through a single path of emotion. So most religions grew up on this, and they cranked it up to the next level and called it 'devotion'.

What you call devotion is an unreasonable emotion. You cannot put it to reason. If you dissect it logically and see, it looks all stupid. But for the person who is going through it, it is fantastic. The same with love affairs. Love affairs are always stupid. Logically, if you apply your intellect and see, it is stupid; but without love, your life is not worthwhile, isn't it?

So love is not to be logically dissected and seen, because emotion cannot be subject to reason. It is a certain aspect of you. At the same time there is a reason behind it because the way you think is the way you feel. Now if you think this is a very wonderful person, you will have sweet emotions towards that person. If you think this is a horrible person, you will have nasty emotions towards that person. You cannot think this is a horrible person and have sweet emotions, or this is a very beautiful person and have nasty emotions. It is not possible because the way you think is the way you feel.

Your emotions are just the juicier part of your mind. This longing to become one with something is always happening on all levels. If it finds expression in a very basic physical way, we call this either food or sex. Food and sex are just this — you want to make something a part of yourself. You try as hard as you want, it does not work. You seem to get there, but then you fall apart. If you find a mental expression to this, it is generally labeled 'greed' or 'conquest' in society. You are trying to make something which is not you become part of you. You do it by acquiring knowledge, or power, or property, or any other thing. You are trying to make something a part of yourself. This is a mental expression. If it finds an emotional expression, you call it love or devotion, because what is the object of the devotee? He wants to become one with his object of devotion. What is the object of love? It is to become one with the person whom you think you love.

So, the same thing is happening on all levels; you are longing to be a little more than what you are, that is all. If you find physical expression, it goes this way; if you find mental expression, it goes that way; if you find emotional expression, it goes a third way. All these things can be inspiring factors to growth, but none of these things are an end by themselves. They cannot take you to the goal because love is an endless longing; you never achieve the oneness. At many moments you think you are one, but the next moment it is not so. Do you not have enough experience with life? Do you still believe it is going to happen?

So, these different expressions are fine; they are beautiful, but they will not find fulfillment. They are very sweet, but they will not find fulfillment, and can turn very bitter. So because we see that expression through the physical body or through the mind or through the emotion does not find fulfillment, we are working upon your energies. With this, you can very easily find fulfillment, because here you do not need anybody else's cooperation. If you want to physically fulfill this, or mentally fulfill this, or emotionally fulfill this, you need the cooperation of the whole world in some way. But energy-wise, if you want to fulfill it, you do not need anybody's cooperation; it is just you.

You are the only reliable person on the planet, isn't it? No matter who is around you, certain moments of doubt will come, but you are the only person about whom you never have doubts because you know you can rely upon yourself for your well-being. At least you know you will not let yourself down. So if you go the energy way, fulfillment will come much more easily because you do not need anybody's cooperation. With everything else you need so many people's cooperation. That is why kriya yoga has been considered the wisest, because if you practice it you do not need anybody's cooperation.

So, is love a natural longing within a human being? The longing is to become one. If you look at it in a simple way, it functions as a desire. Whether you desire food, or sex, or love, or God, or heaven or whatever, it is still a desire, is it not? The root is in the desire. The root of your love is in the desire, yes? The root of your hunger and sexuality, and ambition and your spiritual longing — everything is rooted in desire. And desire is only the longing to expand and include something else as part of yourself.

So is love a natural longing? No. Desire is a natural longing. Love is an emotional expression to that desire. And a certain part of you is emotion, you cannot deny it. A certain amount of your life energies are allotted to your emotion. You have to expend that. Otherwise it will sit in your belly like a stone.

See, there is something called prarabdha. Prarabdha means the allotted karma for this lifetime. In this, there are different volumes, or different percentages in different people. Prarabdha karma is allotted to different activities; some is allotted to physical activity, some to mental activity, and some to emotional activity. The proportion of allotment differs from person to person. That is why people look so different, because this allotment is very different. In one person there is so much mental activity; in another person so much emotional activity; and in yet another person so much physical activity. This is simply because of the volume of energy allotted, according to their prarabdha. So a certain amount of energy is allotted to your emotions.

Today, in the modern world, I find most people — I would say ninety percent of the people — somehow do not find full expression for their emotions. This is probably because the emotional relationships have become so unstable in the world that they do not get to really express themselves. Those of you who are going into the Bhava Spandana program will find it is a complete and thorough overhaul of your emotional energy. It sets it to the highest pitch so that emotion does not stand in the way of your life. You experience the peak of your emotion, not for anything or anybody; it simply turns up your emotional energy.

We can do this to your body also; we can do this to your

mind and to your energies also. If you are in controlled conditions, we could do this to your body in a beautiful way. We can tune your physical body to its ultimate limit, and everything that the body can experience — the deepest pleasures of the body — will just happen to you without anybody's help. Much, much more than you have ever imagined will happen to the body without anybody's help. It could happen to you just where you are sitting now.

The same can happen to your mind. The deepest sense of joy and ecstasy in the mind will happen without anybody's help. You will see, the same will happen with the emotions. But these things need controlled conditions, because if you just let people loose like that, they could fall off the track very easily. So we do it in controlled conditions.

Emotion is a much safer thing to handle than the mind or the body because of various factors. One factor is because people do not have the necessary discipline either in their minds or in their bodies. If they had a little more discipline in their bodies and minds, we could tweak everybody up so that they could walk the streets in full pleasure. I would like to see that kind of world.

⟼⟜

"Whenever you are deeply involved, you become aware. When you are being fanatical, there is no possibility of awareness."

Questioner: How can one be totally involved and yet not become fanatical?

Sadhguru: See, without involvement there is no life. Unless you are involved in something, you will not know life at all. You will remain aloof, and you will not experience anything in your life. If you want to know something, you must involve yourself; otherwise, there is no life. Involvement and fanaticism are not connected in any way. Somebody becomes a fanatic because he fundamentally believes something which is not even in his experience, and above all, he thinks everybody else in the world must be wrong.

Involvement does not demand fanaticism. You can be involved in something not because you believe it is absolutely right, but because you see that it works for you. Because it works for you, you want to put in more involvement so that it works on a deeper level for you; that is all. As it works more and more, your involvement also deepens more and more. But without involvement there is no possibility for anything. Even if you want to digest the food that you eat, you need involvement.

To people who simply gulp food, food does not do the same

thing to them as to people who eat it with involvement. You try one meal like this, and one meal the other way, and you will see how the quantity of food drops if you eat it with involvement. With your being totally involved every moment with the food that is being chewed in your mouth, you will see that the quantum of food will drop to one-fourth of what you usually eat. That is all the food you actually need. You eat the other three quarters because you do not even know that you are eating.

Involvement will naturally bring awareness. Whenever you are deeply involved, you become aware. When you are being fanatical, there is no possibility of awareness. When you lose all your awareness, you become fanatical, isn't it? So these two things are almost diametrically opposite. I do not know how you connect the two. Your idea of involvement is in terms of taking to the streets and shouting slogans; it is not that. Out of your involvement you can do anything that is needed; that is all. You will do anything that is needed; you do not need to believe in something that drives you in a direction which is opposed to everything else around you.

Involvement just puts you in line with what you wish to do and brings awareness into your life, and into whatever little things that you do. If you do something without involvement, you will do it in an unaware way.

Fanaticism means being totally unaware of what you are doing, but it fires you up and gives you a different level of confidence. A fanatic is very confident and very clear; He has no doubts. Involvement does not necessarily mean clarity.

Clarity has to be earned. Clarity which comes from vision, clarity which comes from perception, has to be earned. It will not just come free. But the clarity that comes with fanaticism is free. As a fanatic, you just have to say "this is it," and you are clear-headed about it because you do not see the other things.

If you do not see anything else, and you just see your way as the only way, then that kind of clarity is destructive. Clarity should allow you to flow through your life effortlessly. Clarity should also allow life around you to happen at its best. If you are very clear about what life is, you will ensure that life around you happens beautifully. But a fanatic's clarity is not like this. It comes in a single track of the mind; it does not consider the other tracks. But the more involved you get, the more thoughtful you become. A whole process begins with your involvement, because you cannot do anything now without considering everything.

So, involvement is something that enhances life. Fanaticism is something that narrows down and limits your life. A fanatic can perform actions that nobody else can perform. Fanatical groups can do tremendous things! What they can do is tremendous because they place no full-stops anywhere. They have removed all blocks; they are all out, but on a single track. Having multi-channel music going on a single track is very different. With a single track everything seems to be clear, but that is not real clarity. It is a distorted perception if you think that just by looking through a keyhole, you have seen the world.

❧

"Anybody who performs actions without being aware of the consequences will live his life foolishly."

Questioner: Most of the time we are told that all the good things in life are illegal, immoral or fattening. We live with this continuous contradiction in our lives. We also do things in pursuit of happiness, but we end up in misery. Why are we subjected to this trap? If there is a way to access inner joy, why it is so abstract in nature that people like us, who have a certain basic intelligence, are continuously falling astray?

Sadhguru: Now, you are talking about it as if somebody set a trap. Nobody set a trap. You set it, and you walk into it. Just look at every stage, every step, and every moment of your life. Whatever you do, whether consciously or unconsciously, you are making a choice. Sometimes you choose consciously, and many times unconsciously, but you are making the choices. You are setting the whole thing up. Yes, there are other forces functioning, of course; that is part of living in the world. But fundamentally, how you are within yourself is definitely decided by you.

So you want to know why there is a trap, why this blissfulness is so difficult to attain, and why it is not available to people like you. Who told you it is not available? It is available. It is just that you got too enamored by the outside situation, and you are still not yet tired of it.

Now you say all the good things in life are sins or least fattening. It is not so. There is no good thing in life, and there is no bad thing in life. You do whatever you want to do. It is just that for everything that you do, there is a consequence. If you do something today, you should not cry tomorrow when you see the consequence. If you can joyfully go through the consequence, do whatever you want. But if you are going to cry over the consequences, be careful about your actions. That is all.

So there is no such thing as good or bad. It is you who decide whether something is good or bad. But for every action that you perform, there is a consequence. Anybody who performs actions without being aware of the consequences will live his life foolishly. If you are aware of the consequences and still you do the actions, then when the consequences come, there should be no problem, isn't it?

PART THREE

COMPLETION:

Truth, Life, the Master

"When you know the pain of ignorance; when you really know the pain of ignorance, then a master arises."

Spirituality is like anything else in your life. Usually in your life, when you are done with one thing, the next thing begins. Just the same way, when you are done with everything else, the spiritual process begins. When you look at the basics of life, you find spirituality is very much like sexuality. For example, when you became fourteen, suddenly all those little things that meant the world to you as a child, like your teddy bear, are thrown in the dustbin. The teddy bear goes into the trash can, and all the childish games disappear.

When a certain level of awareness arises in you, you suddenly know that little games do not satisfy you anymore. When you reach fourteen, what you thought important until then has become petty; suddenly it does not mean much to you. You have found the 'big things'. When everything becomes petty in your life, you are turning spiritual. The so-called big things in your life become petty when spirituality arises. There, the hormones in you are a sign of maturity; here it is only awareness which can induce this maturity.

When you have the awareness to see through various activities of life, the various compulsions of life, the various longings of life, when you see them as simply an endless rigmarole which does not really lead you to anything in particular, then the spiritual process can begin. You are in these endless games for fifty to sixty years and they have not moved you an inch towards something meaningful. Either you go through life and realize it on your deathbed, or you realize it as you begin life, or you realize it when you are in the middle of your life and still have time on your hands. So the spiritual process has to begin somewhere, but the longing to go beyond the limitations in which you live is always there.

Every little thing in our lives, when we are fully into it, seems like it is everything, isn't it? From eating what we want, to doing what we want, to relationships and all those things – whenever we are into any of these activities, it looks like it is the be-all and end-all of life. If we rise a little above and look at them, suddenly they all become such petty things, and we wonder, "Why the hell are we in this?"

So when this question begins to rise – "Why am I stuck in all these little things?" – then the spiritual process has begun. Unfortunately, most people endure their spirituality unconsciously. I say 'endure' because when you unconsciously seek the highest truth, it is going to put you through all kinds of nonsense in your life. You really have to have great endurance to be able to go through everything – from having a big breakfast to shopping in a mall and getting married or whatever else. After all, everybody is seeking fulfillment, is it not? Whether you are seeking fulfillment consciously or unconsciously, that is the only difference.

Truth is not a conclusion. Truth is not somewhere you go. It is not a destination; it is just a living experience. You cannot get to truth. You can never get to truth but you can become truth. If you drop all your nonsense, you are truth. If you drop all your limitations, you are that; but you can never get there. It is not a conclusion. You just become truth. If you are willing to see life, experience life beyond all the limitations that you have gathered in the process of life, then you are truth.

Probably the English word, 'truth', creates a whole lot of misunderstanding, because if you talk about truth you will have to talk about untruth. So the English word 'truth' does not really say it. An appropriate word would be in the Sanskrit language where there is something called 'rithambhara'. Or, when one is in that state it is called 'rithambhara pragna'. One who is aware of rithambhara is rithambhara pragna. Ritha means 'that which is the foundation of everything'. The cosmic basis of life is ritha. Whatever nonsense you believe yourself to be, fundamentally you are life, is it not?

If you are life, the basis of life must definitely be somewhere accessible to you. Whether it is rooted here, or in the sky, or anywhere else, it must be rooted somewhere, isn't it? It must be connected; that which is life must always be in touch with the source of what it is. Getting to the very source of who you are is truth. It is always there; it is just that it is covered up with the heap that you have gathered in the form of your body and your mind.

So this process of seeking the ultimate is simple, but at the same time, most human beings on the planet unfortunately experience it as the most complex and impossible process. This is simply because what you are looking for is hidden within you. When I say 'you', I mean the things that you are identified with right now — in your own body, in your own mind, in whatever you experience as 'myself'. And all that you have gathered in the form of body, or in the form of mind, is always focused on the outward. Right now, all the faculties, every aspect of what you know as 'myself', is all outward-bound.

So, let's say the longing has risen within you that you want to know, you really want to know. I know this wanting to know sometimes bubbles up and again gets lost in the daily rigmarole. The nature of the mind and the body is such, even the simplest processes of life could be greatly entangling. Simple things, such as getting up in the morning, rolling up the blinds, brushing your teeth, using the toilet, eating breakfast, going to work, all these little things can be highly entangling. From the moment you wake up to the time you finish your breakfast, which is just a question of an hour or two, you are at the peak of agitation, isn't it? Nothing has happened yet; no calamities have struck yet; you have not met your boss yet, you know; (*Laughs*) nothing has happened. You just saw your wife, or your husband, or maybe your children. You know all your children's tricks. You've been with them for a few years; you know all their tricks; nothing will surprise you, isn't it? But before you reach the breakfast table or before you get up from it, you are at the peak of agitation. This is not because there is something wrong with your life; nothing has gone wrong yet in the day. It is simply because that is the nature of the mind. If you allow it to rule you, that is how you go; there is no other way. It does not matter whether life situations are going well or not going well.

So if this is the nature of the mind, and this is the way life goes on, it is definitely time for people to look at the very nature of their lives from a much deeper perspective, and with a much deeper penetration. The time has come. Most people do not realize that the time has come; they think they can do it next year. They think they can do it after two years; there is no such thing. If you value your life, the time has come; only if you do not value your life, the time hasn't come. If you have any value for this life and this creation, then the time has definitely come, and you must look at life with its ultimate perspective.

If the longing genuinely arises in you, when your heart really cries wanting to know, when you really know the pain of ignorance, then a master arises. You do not have to look for him because if your longing to know has really picked up a certain intensity, and if the pain of ignorance has really gone deep into you, then a master will happen.

I need to say this: I have initiated more people that I have never physically met than the people that I have met. There is a disadvantage, a handicap, when I initiate people I meet physically. When you see the other person is also a person like you – who has a body like you, eats like you, speaks like you – it is a disadvantage because you cannot help but judge him. You cannot help but be protective of yourself; you cannot help but do all those usual things that happen when you meet people around you. So it has always happened that you start with a handicap.

This is the unfortunate reality; most of the time, it is only after the spiritual masters have left that their methods, their processes, and their teachings pick up momentum. When they were still there, it very rarely happened. Their methods pick up momentum only after they have left because suddenly you do not have to battle with their personality anymore. You know, dead people are always convenient. (*Laughter*)

Almost all the time, huge spiritual waves happen after the master is physically dead. When he was physically alive, you had problems, problems, and problems. It does not matter how much experience happened at so many different moments, one word or one action that you did not like was enough to make a wall arise. And very few masters had the freedom to do what they pleased, or whatever they saw as right. Most masters had to work with the existing values of the society, with the existing moralities, with the existing nonsense around them. Within that, there is very little you can do; there is very little possibility. Within the limitations of your understanding, if you seek the ultimate there is very little possibility.

So when you carry a handicap intentionally, it is like this. One day, two men were hunting in the forest. One was carrying a large wooden cage; the other was carrying a concrete pole. They were plodding across. Both the things they were carrying were heavy, and difficult to manage, especially since they were walking in the forest. After some time, the guy with the concrete pole asked, "Why are you carrying this wooden cage?"

"If a wild animal attacks me, I will just get into the cage and I will be safe." (*Laughter*)

They walked on; they were really struggling through the forest. Then the other guy asked, "Why are you carrying a concrete pole?"

"When a wild animal attacks me, I can drop the concrete pole and run faster." (*Laughter*)

So, have you come here with a concrete pole or with the cage? (*Laughs*) People drag their feet for different reasons, but most people do drag their feet.

It happened once on Time Square – you know these things can happen only there. One man was dragging his right foot as he walked. Then another man came in the opposite direction; he was also dragging his right foot. The first man looked at the other and thought, "Okey, one more guy dragging his right foot." As they came closer to each other, the first guy looked at the other, pointed to his right leg and said, "1968, Vietnam." The other man pointed at his right leg and said, "Dog sheet, twenty feet away."

So the reasons why you are dragging your feet may vary, but when you are dragging your feet you do not walk well, and you do not reach where you have to go.

Whatever you choose, you should choose when you are aware, alert, and not entangled; whatever you choose, you should choose when your intelligence is functioning with some sense of clarity. That is what you should go after in your life. When you are embroiled in something, when you are entangled in something, your mind, your body and everything around you says something else; that is not how it should be. And the nature of your mind is such that every day it says different things, isn't it? This is because what you consider to be your mind has nothing to do with you. It is an accumulation of what you gathered from outside. Because you gathered so many bits and pieces, it speaks in bits and pieces.

Please see this. Most minds — I would say 99.9% of the minds in the world — can only speak sense in bits. Continuous dialogue is always absolute nonsense. What goes on continuously in your mind is something that is happening because you are deeply entangled with things. You only make sense in bits and pieces at certain moments, because the process of gathering has always been from outside and in bits and pieces. No matter how much you try to integrate it into one whole, it never happens. If you learn how to keep the mind aside, then there is a continuous stream of sense flowing from beneath the mind, from beyond the mind. But from the mind, continuous sense can never come. It can only come in flashes.

These flashes can be an inspiration, but can never offer guidance. You can never depend on a light which goes on and off, to walk somewhere, can you? If it is on, then you can walk. An on-and-off light can be just an inspiration to tell you, "Okay, there is something called light." But that light is no good; it will not make a good torchlight for you; it just goes on and off at its own will. It just tells you there is something called light which is worth pursuing, that is all.

"All you want to do is be joyful and blissful within you, but you want to go around the world and get there...If it is within you, all you have to do is turn around and face it."

Questioner: This question is about self-realization. How do you get there?

Sadhguru: Oh. You are asking a very big question, very casually. (*Laughs*) Why do you want to be self-realized? To be happy?

Questioner: Yes.

Sadhguru: So let us address the issue directly. Whether you are trying to make money, or you are trying to make a name for yourself, or you are building your family, or you are going to the temple, or you are going to the bar — everything you do is in pursuit of happiness. Somebody thinks the way to happiness is through heaven; another thinks it is through the food plate. Somebody else thinks happiness is through the bottle, another thinks it is through having a husband, a wife, or a child. Everybody is trying to get there in so many different ways. Now your way is self-realization. I think it is time we addressed it directly.

In the world around, you may be identified with many, many things, but at this moment, when you are just sitting here, if you look at yourself, you are just a certain amount of life energy. See, you think, "I am a man," "I am a woman," "I am this," "I am that," in reference to something. But in your experience of life, at this moment, if you simply sit here, the world disappears. Right now you are just a certain amount of life energy, and you are functioning as such.

This life energy, which you call 'myself' right now, has it sometimes been joyful? Sometimes it has been very joyful; sometimes it has been utterly miserable. It has sometimes been peaceful, sometimes very disturbed. It has sometimes experienced agony, at other times experienced ecstasy. So, this life energy is capable of all these things. Your life energies are capable of both — agony and ecstasy, misery and joy, peace and turmoil. It is capable of all this.

If you had a choice as to what kind of expression your life energies should find right now, what would you choose: agony or ecstasy?

Questioner: Ecstasy.

Sadhguru: That much intelligence you have. That much intelligence everybody has. Nobody has to teach you any philosophies, like "Please choose joy, do not choose misery." Do you need scriptures like this? No, because the very life in you is longing to be joyful. This is not somebody's idea that you must be happy. The very life in you is longing to be joyful. So, wanting to be joyful is not somebody's goal, not somebody's idea, not somebody's philosophy. It is the longing of life itself to be in a certain way. As a flower wanting to bloom, the life within you is constantly seeking how to be as joyful as it can be, but you are doing everything to defeat that.

If joy is what you are seeking, if ecstasy is what you are seeking, you must just see that you operate your life energies the way you want them; your life energies should function the way you want them to function. If they were, misery would not arise in your life. So that is what you need to do right now. You need to see that your body, your mind, and your life energies function the way you want them to function.

What we call self-realization is not about being happy. You are very blissful, but you want to go beyond that. You are not trying to live your life well. That you have done anyway, but you want to know the very source of life. Only then you talk about self-realization. Right now if you are just trying to live well, do not talk about all this nonsense. Do not talk about God, about self-realization, about all this nonsense, when you are just trying to live well. You just need to learn to use your body, mind and energies properly, and you will live well.

Now suppose living well is not enough for you; you want to know the very source of life. You are even willing to throw away living well in order to know the source of life. This is when you are seeking self-realization, okay? Right now, you are just looking at how to live well. So approach it directly. Why do you want to go through heaven for that? You want happiness, why do you not address it directly? Why do you want to route it through heaven, or anything else for that matter? You had better approach it directly because you have already seen that it is within you. You need not go around the world and come here to realize what is within you.

It happened once that somebody came near the Yoga Center in India, and he asked a local village boy, "How far is it to the Isha Yoga center?"

The boy said, "It is 24,996 miles."

"What, is it that far?"

"Yes, the way you are going, that is how far it is. If you turn around, it is just four miles."

So this is what you are doing to yourself. All you want to do is be joyful and blissful within you, but you want to go around the world and get there. By the time you go around the world you may be dead. You do not have a million-year life-span. Human life is so brief. If you had a million-year life-span, you could go around the world and come; but still that would not make sense. When it is within you, does it make any sense to you to go around the world to be joyful? Only a fool would do that. If it is within you, all you have to do is turn around and face it.

All experiences, whether experiences of misery or ecstasy, are happening within you. So face them. Learn to address your issues directly, not in roundabout ways. Do you have the energy to travel 24,996 miles? No. Most people would die on the way.

"Once you had a glimpse of something, it is foolish to try to jump again and again, to have a glimpse of it. It is time to build a ladder to scale the wall."

Questioner: If someone once reached a certain experience naturally, and he cannot reach it again, what can he do to regain that state?

Sadhguru: Have you been to a prison? Have you been to a military camp? (*Laughs*) If you are behind a wall, in a small area, and you lived your whole life there, you would think that was the world, because you lived within that compound.

Maybe there was a springboard there, or a trampoline, and one day you just jumped up really high, and saw beyond the wall. You saw a whole wide fantastic world out there, but in a moment again you landed in your old spot. And again and again you tried to jump on your trampoline to get that high, but you were unable to get there. It would be quite frustrating.

Once you have had a glimpse of something, it is foolish to try to jump again and again and have a glimpse of it. It is time you built a ladder to scale the wall, isn't it? You had a glimpse; you know it is worthwhile, so what is the point of jumping again and again to have a peep over the wall? Once you know it is worthwhile, you must try to build a step-ladder so that you can climb up across the wall and go there for good.

Jumping up can happen in so many ways for so many reasons; it sometimes may even happen accidentally, but the ladder will not happen accidentally. It needs to be built. You need a technology for building a ladder. That is what we are trying to do. Right now all the yoga that we are trying to teach you is just a way for you to build a ladder where you do not have to jump up to see something. Slowly, step by step, you go up. If you just keep the simple practice every day, I will guarantee you a hundred percent that in a year's time, or in two years' time, your experience of life will be very, very different from what it is right now. This is one hundred percent guaranteed. There is no question about it. If you are doing it properly and keeping it up, you will see the way you experience life, the quality of your life will gradually change without even you noticing. Slowly, step-by-step, it will change, and slowly it will deliver you there.

How long does it take for one to climb? It depends on various factors. All individuals will not climb at the same speed, and they should not. If you try to climb this mountain like somebody else, you may fall down and break your head. You must climb at your own pace. It is okay. Are you climbing to your full potential? That is all that matters.

"Imagination is one freedom you have."

Questioner: What is the role of the imagination in our lives? Is it important to make our imagination pleasant?

Sadhguru: We do not know whether we can make our lives pleasant or not. At least we can make our imagination pleasant, isn't it? If you make your imagination so ugly that you are always seeing terrible things, then we need to work on it. You need a complete overhaul, because imagination is one little freedom that you have. You cannot fly off right now, but you can fly in your imagination. You cannot become a king or a queen right now, but you can become one in your imagination. You cannot, you know, become God right now, but you can become one in your imagination.

Anything you want, you can become in your imagination. Unfortunately, you are using your imagination to create terrible things for yourself.

The other aspects of your life are not so fluid; they are not so much in your hands as your imagination is. Your life situations, your body, your breath, your mind, the other aspects of the mind, are not so much in your hands. Imagination is one thing which is completely in your hands. But even with that, if you create terrible things with it, such as fear, it means you have got a very negative imagination.

There were two identical twins. Between the two of them, the only thing that was identical was their appearance. In everything else they were opposites. One was an out-and-out pessimist; one was a sunshine-in-the-rain optimist. The father of these twins was always confounded as to how to handle them.

So it was the fourteenth birthday for the twins. The father, after much thought, decided to treat the birthday this way: for the doomsday pessimist, he bought all the gifts that he could buy. Every kind of toy, every kind of gift that was available in the shops, he brought and heaped up into his son's room and painted all the walls with 'Happy Birthday, Happy Birthday.'

For the optimistic boy he brought a heap of horse dung and put it in his room. Then he let these boys go to their rooms after dinner. He was very curious to know what would happen. He quietly tiptoed and listened to what was happening in the rooms. He went to the pessimist's room and heard the boy crying his heart out. Not able to bear it, he opened the door and said, "What happened? I bought you all the gifts. I bought you everything that anybody could imagine. Why are you crying?"

The boy, who was really crying his heart out, said, "Now I have to read the instructions for all these toys. The batteries will run out, and every day I have to replace the batteries. My friends will come and steal many of the toys. I have to share the toys with them and many will be broken after some time." Like this he went on; he cried and cried.

The father, feeling absolutely hopeless, consoled the boy and put him to sleep. He walked out of his room, and thought, "Okay, let me see what is happening with the horse dung." If this is what happens with the finest gifts that you give, what should be happening with the horse dung? He went near this boy's room and he heard this boy singing and dancing in the room. He opened the door and saw the boy dancing in the horse dung. He got angry. "What are you dancing about, and in a heap of horseshit?" The boy said, "There must be a pony around." (*Laughs*)

So, at least your imagination can make things pleasant and beautiful. Maybe we cannot change our surroundings or the people around us cannot immediately; maybe we cannot change our politicians or the world situations cannot immediately; but at least our imagination can make things wonderful and beautiful. Imagination is one thing that you have that you can make any way you want. Why are you making it terrible and fearful?

—◦◦◦◦—

"The presence of any guru with the potential to offer something is a blessing...His very presence is a blessing."

Questioner: My son is mentally handicapped. He has Down's syndrome and I often wonder what his potential is for self-realization. He's probably better off than all of us because he's just genuinely happy all the time, but I just wondered what your opinion on that was. How can people like that become self-realized?

Sadhguru: Now, many times you will see that realized people are almost like people with Down's syndrome, but they come from two different dimensions.

The way in which your body functions and the way in which your mind functions has really nothing to do with your self-realization. But to make the effort to go beyond the limitations of body and mind, you must know the pain of the mind. You must know the suffering and frustration of the mind. If you do not know the suffering and frustration of the mind, you will not seek anything beyond that.

Now, a person like what you are describing is in many ways incapable of suffering; so, he will not long for anything beyond. In that way he is incapable. But suppose he suffers — there are other kinds of mental disorders where they suffer immensely — would he be capable of self-realization?

As I said, the function of your mind has nothing to do with your realization. But to get the longing, you must be in a certain level of understanding. Unfortunately, you must be on a certain level of suffering. Or, on a certain level of sharpness of intelligence to be able to say, "Anyway, suffering will come. Right now it has not come. That does not matter. But it can come. It can happen."

Gautama the Buddha lived in absolute pleasure. He was a king. But he saw one sick person, one old person, and one dead body and immediately he said to himself, "All these three things can happen to me any moment. They are inevitable. They are bound to happen." So he started to look beyond.

So to look beyond you must be able to either suffer yourself, or you must be able to perceive other people's suffering as your own and look beyond that. If you are very intelligent, you will not wait till suffering comes to you. If you are not intelligent, you will wait till suffering comes to you. If you are an absolute idiot, no matter how much suffering comes to you, you will only try to appease it; you will try to handle it, and you will not look beyond it.

When a person is mentally ill or incapable or handicapped, he is unable to suffer. Some types of people are unable to suffer. They are just happy for no reason. That is why, if you are simply happy by your own nature, people will say, "You are crazy." They say the same if somebody is simply suffering but he is unaware of his suffering. By 'unaware', I mean that he does not see any other way.

People with other kinds of mental disorders suffer immensely, but they are just not aware of another possibility. If there is suffering and a break, then you understand that you need to go beyond this process of creating suffering. If there is just suffering or just no suffering, you have no perspective to realize that you can go beyond. It is not that you cannot. You can, but you do not have the mental perspective to realize that you have to make an effort to go beyond. So, in that way, it is an incapability. But, in a basic way as a human being, is your son incapable of becoming realized? He is as capable as anybody.

It is just that we could put a certain seed into people with mental disorders and it will anyway find fruit because they will not meddle with the seed. Very easily it will find fruit. Usually they are always blessed.

The presence of any guru with the potential to offer something is a blessing. It is not that he has to look at this person or bless that person. His very presence is a blessing. All those beings who are receptive to it will reap from it. Those who are not receptive to it, we have to put them in this room and grind them through the day. (*Laughs*)

—⊶⊷—

"Memory creates a hallucination of the past. Desire creates a hallucination of the future."

Questioner: I seem to live in past memories. Yet I want to walk the spiritual path. What can I do?

Sadhguru: All memories create a past for us, and make it more real than reality. For many of you the bank of memory that you carry is much more important to you than what is happening to you now. "No, I cherish my past." You do not cherish your past. You are full of fear so you cling to the past. So memory creates a hallucination of the past. Desire creates a hallucination of the future.

As your societies have encouraged you, most individuals have misunderstood desire to be courage. When you glorify a simple misunderstanding of life as something big, naturally you get trapped in it. If fear rules, you will see that the past will be very important for you. But if desire rules you, the future will be very important for you, and life that is here becomes unimportant.

When an individual is not an individual but a whole mess of nonsense that he has gathered from the past, then this is the way life happens: either he clings to the past, when he is afraid, or when he feels a little brave, he has desires about the future. He is never in this moment. All of creation and the creator is in this moment, but the engine of life for most people is sustained or demolished by the process of memory and desire.

I want you to understand this. When I sit here and speak, I see many people nodding their heads as if they agree with everything that I say. They do not agree with me. It is just that what I am saying agrees with something of their past. There are some people here who find that what I am saying does not agree with their past, nor with their sensibilities, so they are just trying to be as expressionless as possible. There are some others who find that what is being said is utterly true, but the truth seems to be threatening, so they look glum and morose. Every time such people sit with me, it feels like we are in a funeral. (*Laughter*) I sit here peeling away life; I am peeling away all the things that you hide within yourself and all the bull that you call as secret; I am peeling it away because the peel just does not matter.

It happened once. Shankaran Pillai parked his car and went into the supermarket. He was planning to go in for just five minutes. He went in, but then he met a friend, and it took a little more time, and then he came out. There he saw a motorcycle cop writing a parking ticket. He went up to him and he said, "You pencil-neck idiot, why are writing a ticket?" The policeman just looked at him and started writing the second ticket for bald tires. Then Shankaran Pillai abused him again. The policeman wrote one more ticket. Shankaran Pillai abused him again; he wrote one more ticket.

This went on for a full twenty minutes. Then his friend pulled him away and asked, "What are you doing to yourself? Do you know what all those tickets can do to you?" He said, "I do not give a damn. My car is parked across the corner." (*Laughter*)

So, that is how it seems to all of you: 'my car is parked across the corner'.

I want you to understand. If you wish to walk into a dimension which is not in your present level of experience and understanding, there are a few ways in which you can enter it. One thing is I give you the road map, and you find your way. It is up to you. So, when you are trying to go into a dimension beyond your understanding and experience using a road map, you could get lost. A road map is good but, you know, with the road map you are all the time lost, isn't it? Even in the United States, if you use a road map you get lost. (*Laughs*)

A second way would be when I put my tail lamps on and say, "Just follow me." Now you try to keep up a certain pace, but suddenly fog comes, and you do not see my tail lamp any more. You immediately say, "Oh, this guy ditched me. I trusted him, but no, this is not it." Then again you see a glimmer of the tail lamp and you think, "Oh yes, it is okay." (*Laughter*) This keeps on happening and sometimes between traffic, there are ten cars between you and me, and then again you think, "Oh, he left me." That is how it is when you are following.

A third way is, you just get into my bus and sit. Once you get into my bus, even if you doze off, it does not matter. Anyway you will go to the destination, but then you cannot drive.

So these are the three ways. I am game for any of them. If you are the adventurous kind, you take the road map. If there is no adventure in you but you want to act brave, then we will keep the tail lamps on. Most people who claim to be adventurous always avoid every possibility of adventure. Is it not so? Just look carefully. Every opportunity that you have in your life to be adventurous, you make sure you somehow avoid it.

Or you are just tired of getting lost. Here, you do not care to prove anything to anybody or to yourself. You just get into the bus and plunk yourself; it goes where it has to go. You choose. I'm not compelling you into anything. It is okay with me. If you have lots of time, play along with the roadmap. If you are in a hurry, you can hop onto the bus.

Now this is neither easy nor difficult. It is just simple. However, your mind which is being pulled and pushed by so many factors — your mind which is functioning within the limitations that you have gathered, your mind in which many of your limitations are gold-plated — is making it all that confusing. That is all.

If you stop gold-plating your limitations, if you stop seeing the shackles that you wear as ornaments, it is very simple. But you are on a full-time deception game with yourself and all the time, you talk about this deception to seek support from everybody around you. Please see in how many ways you are seeking support for your limitations from people around you. You want approval for your limitations. Everybody says yes, yes, it is so. Any number of times, I hear people sitting with me for a few days and then saying, "When we go back to the real world..." (*Laughter*) Oh, I did not know I was in the unreal world. I thought I am more in reality than anybody else. (*Laughs*)

Once there was an old lion. This lion was prowling, looking around for grub. A fat old bull had strayed into the forest. The lion saw it and he thought, "This is it." He was just looking for a snack, but here there was a whole meal. You know a bull is not like other animals of the forest; it is easy prey. So with great joy, the lion pounced upon the bull, killed him, and ate him up. With his belly full, full to the point of bursting, he felt really satisfied and he roared. A few hunters were walking in the forest, and they heard the roar. They tracked down the lion and shot him dead. So the moral of the story is, when you are full of bull, do not open your mouth. (*Laughter*)

So, if you are serious about your spiritual path, you can talk about work, about politics, about cinema, but you do not talk about your life. You question your life, but never make statements about your life. The very fact that you say, "I am on the spiritual path," means you have already admitted that, "I do not know a damn thing about myself." Yes? So when you do not know a damn thing about yourself, you do not talk about yourself, or your life.

If you just shut your mouth about yourself and your life, you will see the path becomes so much clearer and easier. When you are full of bull (*Laughs*), you only question life all the time. Never make statements about it.

❦

"Life does not need meaning because it is so complete by itself."

Questioner: What can you say about the role of humanity on this planet? Do we have a role? Is there any meaning to our lives?

Sadhguru: What is the role of humanity? What role can you have except that of life? To be alive in the most exuberant possible way is the fundamental thing that you can do; in fact, it is the only thing you can do. To live and to live totally is all that one can do. There is nothing else.

You may have many, many ideas about yourself, but fundamentally you are just a piece of life. The only thing you can do is raise this aliveness to the highest pitch. The best thing that you can do to yourself and for humanity and for the whole planet is raise this aliveness to its maximum pitch. Become absolutely alive. That is all you can do, and that is more than enough.

Questioner: There is no meaning then?

Sadhguru: You want a meaning?

Questioner: Your idea about it ...

Sadhguru: See, the mind is always looking for a meaning. Life has no meaning. It is beyond all meaning. Life does not need meaning because it is so complete by itself. Logically, you cannot make any sense out of it, but still, it is so complete by itself. Philosophers are always trying to explain life, but they are trying to explain that which cannot be explained.

It is like this. Once there was a rich man who had a young beautiful daughter. Everything was fine about her; she was beautiful; she was healthy; she was wonderful; she was everything. She just had one problem, like most of you. (*Laughs*) Everything is okay with you, but you have just one problem. If you solve that one problem, the next one will be there. So she just had one problem. Her problem was that every day when she woke up in the morning, she became sick. She needed to puke in the morning.

So the father, who was very concerned about his only beautiful daughter, took her to a wise man and told him, "See, my daughter is a wonderful girl; she is beautiful, she is young, everything, but she gets sick in the morning. Is there something we can do?"

The wise man looked at the girl and asked, "Do you give milk to this girl?"

The rich man said, "Yes, the best milk! Not dairy milk, but milk from a particular cow which gives the best milk in town. That is the milk we give our girl."

The wise man said, "That is the problem."

"What do you mean? We are giving her the best milk, and you say that is the problem?"

The wise man said, "Yes, that is the problem. See, she drinks milk before going to bed at night. Before that she has had yogurt. So in her stomach, everything becomes yogurt or curd. (*Laughter*) Then, she is young, so she rolls around in bed. Because of this, this curd gets churned and becomes butter. This butter melts because of body heat and becomes ghee; this ghee, in turn, becomes sugar and this sugar becomes alcohol. No wonder she has a hangover in the morning."

It is a fantastic explanation. So this is how philosophies are; they have fantastic explanations about that which cannot be explained, and that which can only be experienced. Life cannot be explained; it can only be experienced. Life comes only with experience; the deeper your experience of life, the closer you are to life. If you try to find meanings, you will go away from life. People, who have found meanings to life, have always moved away from life. Only by experience you will be in it, because life is not for you to explain or find meanings for. Life is for you to experience and explore to the deepest core. How deep you go, that is how fulfilled you are. If you go to its utmost core, you will be dissolved; nothing of you will exist anymore.

"You are the way you are only because of yourself, nobody else but yourself."

Questioner: Sadhguru, why are people not born aware? Why do they have to struggle to remove the veil in order to know themselves?

Sadhguru: They were born aware, but they have made themselves unaware. Now they are struggling to make themselves aware again.

Questioner: What makes them unaware?

Sadhguru: Themselves.

Questioner: There is another self in them?

Sadhguru: No, yourself.

Questioner: By their own will?

Sadhguru: You. Do not talk about others. What made you unaware? You did. Did somebody else make you unaware or aware? Right from day one since the day you ended up in the Isha Yoga Introductory, we have been constantly trying to point at you, because you are trying to scatter yourself all over the place so that you can never be recovered. If you say I am unaware because my father was a drunkard, or I am unloving because my mother was like that, or I am not intelligent because my teacher was like that, then you are finished. Look at your life now. Your parents are divorced; your teacher is dead, and if we want to change you, we have got to recover all those guys.

Now, you are the way you are only because of yourself, nobody else but yourself. If you see this you can make yourself what you want right now. Instead of lamenting over something that happened or something you imagined happened in the past, try to do something about yourself.

So in the East, in India at least, enlightened beings are referred to as 'dwijas'. Dwija comes from 'ja' which means 'born' and 'dwi which means 'twice'. So dwija means 'twice born'. An enlightened being is born twice. Everybody is born once.

When you are born, you are just fine as a piece of life; you are bubbling with life, and you are just fine. Then you screw yourself up badly. Then you kill that nonsense and you are once again born. Now you are enlightened. When you were a child, though you were just fine, your life then was not self-created. Nature gave it as a gift to you. What is given to you as a gift can only be enjoyed for a certain time. What can be given can be taken away, isn't it?

Now, the second time you are born, you are not born out of your mother's womb, but out of your own awareness. You re-birthed yourself. If you have to be born again, the first thing is you must be willing to die the way you are right now. That is what we have been trying to do for the last three days; we have been trying to somehow kill the way you are right now so that something new can happen.

So an enlightened being is called a dwija or a 'twice born'. But now, this is a self-created birth. Nobody can take this away. What nature gave you can be taken away, but now you gave birth to yourself. This cannot be taken away by anybody or anything. No matter what kind of situation you are placed in, this cannot be taken away. It does not need any insurance backup.

"You can play with creation. You really cannot create anything."

Questioner: How about the creative process? What about wanting to lose yourself in the process? It seems to be partly the desire to create and partly the desire to lose yourself. Which one is it? Is it both, or is it neither?

Sadhguru: Maybe what I am about to say is going to be very insulting to you, but I want you to really look deeper into this. You cannot create anything here. Creation has happened and it is perfect. You can play with creation. You really cannot create anything. Please look at it sincerely. Man may believe that he has created many things, but you are just turning and twisting what is already there.

There is a good joke about this. In the twenty-first century, about fifty years hence, let us say, the scientists of the world met and said, "Now that science has evolved sufficiently we can manage the world on our own. We can create everything ourselves. We created a 'Dolly' and we can create an 'Austin'. We can do whatever we want. We can create life and you know we are already capable of destroying it. So it is time that God retires. Why is he still messing around with us? We can run the world, and we can even create a new world if we want. We can create human beings also, so let him retire."

So a committee of scientists went to heaven, got an appointment with God, met him and said, "Old man, it is time you retired. You have done a good job, all right. But you know at some point everybody's time is up. Everybody retires. It is time you retired. We are capable of doing anything. You know a hundred years ago we created Dolly. Today we can create anything we want."

Then God asked, "Oh, you can create life also?"

"Yes, if you want we will take this mud and make a man out of it." The scientist picked up the mud from the ground and said, "Come on, bring the mobile laboratory. Let us make a man out of this mud."

And God said, "No, no. Make your own mud first."

You are not creating anything. You are just twisting creation this way and that way as it is convenient and useful for you. From the simple caveman who made a pot out of clay to whatever you are making — missiles, rockets, and spaceships — it is still the same process. You are still molding life, molding what is available into different forms, but you are not really creating anything. It is all there. You are just rearranging it a little bit.

So there is no creativity in you. You cannot create. Leave that to the creator. He has done a good job. You can trust him. (*Laughs*) You are just playing with life. When you want to play, play your game in such a way that it is truly enjoyable for yourself and everybody around you. Maybe you cannot liberate them, but at least you can make a joyous situation around you. That itself is liberation in certain ways. Somebody who can be happy all the time, at least he has liberated some parts of his nonsense. He is not absolutely free, but he is free from lots of nonsense.

So let your game be just that. Whatever kind of game you play, let it be about creating joyousness for yourself and the situation around you. Otherwise, you can play any kind of game. If you want you can play a war game, and I am not saying it is right or wrong. It is just that as long as you are shooting somebody, you think it is a great game, but when you get shot, you think it is not a good game. That is not fair. When you want to shoot people you must also be willing to be shot. Only then it is a real game, a fair game.

So if you are not ready for those kinds of games, you should leave them. You want to sing to me, it is fine, but tomorrow if I sing – you know I am not trained like you – you must be able to bear my singing. (*Laughs*)

I am just using these examples for you to see how life is happening: you sing, somebody chatters, somebody does something else. That is their game. That is the only game they know. So you play a game that is conducive for your situation and in some way, if it is not ultimate liberation, at least it frees a few people. When you sing, maybe somebody who has got a hell of a lot of problems in his life, at least for those five minutes, forgets his problems and is happy listening to your song. Let that be your intention.

Now if you can simply sing out of your joy, you do not need any intention. But if that kind of joyousness has not come into you, sing with the intention of creating happiness for somebody. The intention of creating joy for somebody, I would put on a lower scale than you simply bursting forth in joy. It is a lower scale, but it is better than singing for fame. It is better than singing to become somebody in the world. It is better than trying to enhance and establish yourself through your singing. So just see what is possible for you and go by that.

Sing with the intention of being a mother to the world. Maybe somebody thinks your song is a stupid song. It is okay. You sing. Out of your love you sing. If joy is not possible, at least step down to love, caring. Unfortunately, you have placed it the other way around. People think love is much higher than joyousness. If a person is joyous, he need not even be loving. It is fine. His presence is fine. Some of the people who always claim that they love everybody are unbearable, isn't it? (*Laughs*)

———

"You always love dead people because you ...can twist them to your convenience. If you fall in love with the living, this moment there is love; the next moment there is a conflict, the next moment frustration, and the next moment disappointment."

Questioner: You once said an individual does not choose a guru. A guru chooses you. Could you explain this?

Sadhguru: See, if an individual chooses anything, what would he choose? He would choose what is comfortable for him. Please see, you always choose only that which is supportive to your ego. If you choose a friend, what kind of a friend do you choose? You will only choose somebody who supports and enhances your ego. Somebody who keeps poking at your ego, you think that he is not your friend. You will think that he is your enemy.

So, if you start making a conscious choice of a guru, he is not your guru. Whatever he may be, he is not your guru. So please understand, when I say he is not your guru, I am not talking about his state. I am talking about your receptivity. Gautama himself may be sitting here, Jesus may be sitting here, but they cannot do anything to you, unless you are sufficiently receptive.

When Jesus came, how many people could see who he was? Just a handful could. All the others, either they ignored him because he was not worth their attention or they gave him negative attention. They were angry with him. They were upset with him. Very few people experienced him as something else. That is the same reality even now. It has always been the same.

Today, after two thousand years, everybody says "I love Jesus" but it is of no significance. As I have always been telling you, you always love dead people because you know they do not do anything to you. You can twist them to your convenience. Falling in love with the dead is always the best thing because you will never have conflicts. You have a constant love affair. If you fall in love with the living, this moment there is love, but the next moment there is a conflict, the next moment frustration, and the next moment disappointment. So always fall in love with the dead (*Laughs*) because it is so safe and so very fulfilling. Please see that.

Jesus himself never said, "Love me." He said, "Love thy neighbor." Because it is challenging to love the person who is next to you right now, irrespective of who he is. You do not know who the hell he is. You do not know what he is capable of. You do not know what horrible things this man may be doing in his life or what horrible things he may be plotting right now in his mind. But you are still capable of loving this person who is sitting next to you. This is not because you are ignorant of these possibilities. You know all these things are possible, but you are still capable of loving the person next to you, without considering his qualities, his pluses and minuses, the good and evil within him.

If you can do that ninety percent of your spiritual work is done. The remaining ten percent is simple, very easy. You do not have to do anything. We will take care of it for you, if you can just do that.

But you dropped that "Love thy neighbor" and instead made it "Love Jesus." This is easy. This anyone can do. Anyone can love somebody who is not here right now. Unfortunately, this is what we have chosen.

So, it is not a selection that you make. "Okay, I'll go on the website and search for all the gurus in the world — which one, which one, which one?" People are doing it, right? (*Laughs*)

A large group of people from the United States wrote to us in the ashram and said, "We have read something about Sadhguru. We have heard so much about him. We want to come there. We are on the spiritual path. We want to surrender to the master. Our life is about this, but we want to know whether he is a vegetarian or a non-vegetarian."

I was in Lebanon then and from the ashram they sent this mail to me, and they said, "They are asking whether you are a vegetarian, please tell us." You know, these are the people who are in the ashram. They have been with me for years, and they still do not know whether I am a vegetarian or a non-vegetarian, and for them it has never occurred to ask. Whether I am a vegetarian or a cannibal, it does not make any difference to them. Whether I am eating grass or human flesh will not make any difference to them. That is why they never bothered to ask.

So they replied to this US group and said, "See, this is not the way to come to a master. This is not about him. It is about the way you come. If you feel this is going to be useful to you, you come." And that person who sent the mail from the ashram added, "This is everything for me. This has changed my life. I never bothered to ask him what he eats, or what he does, or where he goes, because it is not important for me. The experience has made this kind of difference in me. Please come and do not worry about what he is eating or not eating."

But these people still wanted to know whether he is a vegetarian or not. So I said, "Every moment whatever I breathe, whatever I eat, whatever I drink, I am consuming so many microbes, so I must be a non-vegetarian. You tell them that." Moreover, I told them to say, "If you are going to invite him to your house for dinner — if that is the intention behind your question — he does not eat meat, but he eats seafood."

After that, I think one note came saying that we consider seafood as non-vegetarian so we do not want to have anything to do with this. (*Laughs*) That is it. So, this is not just about diet. This is about so many other things. If you are the one choosing your guru, you will definitely make a wrong choice because you will choose that which supports you.

You just create a longing within you to know. Then you will see that you will get sucked into something helplessly — not because of you, in spite of you. Even though at many points you thought, "This is not it; I must go away," you have been simply drawn into it helplessly. Do not worry about who your guru is. You just see how to intensify your longing and your seeking. What has to happen will happen. A tree can be your guru. A rock can be your guru.

Now do not go about sitting in front of the trees and seek. What I am telling you is that this does not work the way you think. That is why I say if you went to somebody and you experienced something a little beyond yourself — not in terms of feeling more secure, but in terms of breaking your limitations; if you are neither solaced nor made comfortable and if you are uncomfortable with the person but still you want to be there — then that is a good place for you to stay.

"Only if you are on the path of bhakti or devotion, you walk joyously. The intellectual path is always a painful process."

Questioner: At Bhava Spandana you asked us what we wanted and I said ecstasy, but that is not what I am experiencing. I am in a lot of pain a lot of the time, and I feel like an impostor sometimes...

Sadhguru: You are an impostor; it's not just that you feel like one. You are an impostor because you are pretending to be something other than what you actually are. There is nothing new about it. Do not be shocked at being an impostor. It is okay. You are one, but now you have a desire to go beyond that. That is all.

Whatever you see within yourself — the ugliest dimension that you see within yourself — indicates that you are growing. The more ugliness you see, the more aware you have become. You are beginning to see it, that's all. Whether you like it or not, it is there. If you see it, then naturally you will grow. If you do not see it, it means you are deeply embroiled in it.

But you are talking about this impostor in a different context. Now your issue is, "I am not ecstatic, so I am an impostor"...

Questioner: Or just joyous. I'll take joyous...

Sadhguru: Okay. You are not even joyous.

Questioner: Right, not all the time.

Sadhguru: Not all the time... (*Laughs*) Now, if I am not joyous it does not mean I am an impostor. It just means that I am becoming aware of my limitations, which bother me, with which I am still struggling. It is okay. Please become aware of all the limitations.

Although it need not necessarily be so, the spiritual process most of the time, for most people, is a very painful process, because of the way your mental make up is. But it need not be so. It won't be so only when you follow the path of surrender.

If you can just walk away with one single "Come, follow me," only then you walk without pain. Otherwise, giving birth to yourself is a painful process. You know even your physical birth was a painful process to somebody. So giving birth to yourself is a very painful process. Demolishing yourself is an even more painful process.

Only if you are on the path of bhakti or devotion, you walk joyously. The intellectual path is always a painful process. But I am not asking you for devotion, because the moment that word is uttered, immediately you will move into deception. Everybody will think "Yes, we are all 'I love Jesus'." You know, the same thing will happen. You love only to the point of convenience. You will just convert this "I love Jesus" into "I love Sadhguru." Let me tell you this: "I love Sadhguru" exists only to the point of convenience. If he starts stepping everywhere, then "I hate Sadhguru" is just the next step.

So we are not talking about devotion because right now, you do not have the legs to walk that kind of path. So we are going this way painfully. With this, slowly those legs may happen. They will happen. There are many of you who came on the first day of the program with great suspicion. The suspicion deepened in the first four days. You could see the plot, and how it was working. But by the seventh day, from suspicion you moved to being just skeptical. From being skeptical you came to "Okay. I am me, and you are you. But it is all right. It works. This yoga is pretty good. At least my breathing is better. My asthma is better."

Then slowly, as you grow, a point comes — you know for different people it comes at different times — when it does not matter. You feel, "Whatever you do is okay with me." So if those legs become strong then the "Come, follow me" can happen, where you walk joyously. When you walk in devotion, you walk joyously. Otherwise, the spiritual path is a painful process because it is about self-destruction. It is not easy because you built this with so much pain and struggle. To destroy it is even more painful.

See, suppose you want to build a house. You know a lot of pain is involved in making the money, putting the materials together, all that stuff. Suppose tomorrow you are ordered to demolish your own house, the pain is even deeper. Right now that is the situation.

Questioner: I'll go get my bag.

Sadhguru: Oh, a bag? Bags will not pass.

Questioner: I do not want to miss the opportunity, but I do not know what that means.

Sadhguru: Yes, that is what I want you to know. Bags will not pass. Whether it is a leather bag or a body bag, both will not pass.

This bag of flesh and bone will not pass. Only when you keep this bag aside you can really follow. You keep this aside and just see how simple it is to follow me. "Come follow me," does not mean carrying your bags. This head bag also will not go. This body bag also will not go, because these bags you have picked up. On the way you picked up this bag. You have to leave that which does not belong to you.

As long as you carry things that do not belong to you, you are a thief. When you are a thief we will not let you pass through the security gates. If you give up everything that is not you, then you will pass joyously.

—◦◦◦◦◦—

"I am not against pleasure. I am all for pleasure, but I think it is stupid to go for small pleasures. That is all."

Questioner: Sadhguru, what about our needs and desires? Don't we need to fulfill them?

Sadhguru: What is your desire? Just name one.

Questioner: I mean food, sex and sleep.

Sadhguru: Your desire is not about food, sex or sleep. You do not have a desire for sleep. When you have a desire you want to stay awake the whole night, isn't it? So sleep is not on the list of desires. Maybe when you are tired you want to rest, you want to relax, but sleep is not on your desire list.

Food is also not on the desire list. It is a basic requirement. What type of food may be on the desire list, but food itself is not on the desire list. It is much deeper than that. Food is just for your survival. What I should eat tonight may be on the desire list; the variety, the choice is social.

So discounting those two, let us look at the third thing that you mentioned: sexuality. Your desire is not for sex. One part of it is that your intelligence has been hijacked by your hormones. Another part of it is that there is a certain pleasure attached to it. Another part of it is that you are desperately trying to become one with somebody; it is a desperate attempt. You have tried hard, but it does not work. Has it worked? It has not. People are going at it with full vigor thinking they will become one. At that moment, it looks like it is going to happen. It looks like a possibility, but the next moment you know it is not. So either you realize this on your deathbed or you realize it now and look for other ways that may work.

Now, you may ask, "Oh, should I give this up?" There is no need to give up anything. As I said earlier, when you were a child, did you have some kind of a doll of your own? Let us say you had a teddy bear or a Barbie doll, or whatever, something that went all over the world with you.

Now you had this teddy bear with you. At one point in your life this teddy bear was more important than your mother, your father, God, or all of them put together, yes? At a certain point in your life, at that time, suppose I had told you, "See, this teddy bear is just a bundle of cotton. What is the big deal? Let us throw this nonsense away." Would you have listened? No way.

But as you grew up, you saw other things, got interested in many other things. Then where did the teddy bear go which was more precious than anything else in your life? Where did it go? Most of you do not even know where it went, or how it got disposed of. Do you know? Most of you are not even aware. If you had a very meticulous mother, then maybe you know where it is. Otherwise you do not know where the hell it went. Isn't it so?

So something that was so very important for you at one stage in life, at another stage in life, doesn't mean anything. Similarly, right now, you are hanging on to certain teddy bears because you do not know any better. If you taste something bigger, the smaller will just naturally fall off. If you get to know something of a bigger dimension than what you know right now, the little things will naturally fall off. Do you have to give it up? Do you have to renounce it? No, it will just fall off.

Now I am a hundred percent for intoxication. I will vote for intoxication always, but I never drink nor do I take any drugs. I just learned a different way of getting drunk – all the time, at no cost, and with no hangover. It does not cost anything. You can just get drunk anytime and at the same time you can remain fully balanced. You will have no hangovers, and it is good for your health. Is it not a better drink? Is it not better to shift from wine to the divine?

So suppose I taught you a simple technology with which your body is always in extreme pleasure. Do you want it to be touched by somebody now? No, because that somebody will be a disturbance now. You sit here and you are in absolute pleasure — a million times more than what you would know through sexuality. So why would you go for sexuality? The biggest problem with sexuality is that it never lasts, is it not? The biggest frustration for people who are dedicated to sex is just that. For people who do it with a certain amount of love and emotion, for them it may be different. But for people who are dedicated to sex, their greatest problem is that it is too bloody brief. So now if I teach you how to be in it all the time, twenty-four hours a day, with nobody's help, are you interested to learn?

Questioner: Yes.

Sadhguru: So that is why you are in yoga. Just sitting here and breathing is a million times more pleasurable than anything that you have known. There are people who have been to Samyama. They might have not known it all the time, but you can ask them. At certain moments of just breathing — just normally, not even breathing in any particular way, just in and out — ask them what level of pleasure they went into. And breathing is on twenty-four hours a day. If breath can become such a pleasure, why would you go for anything less?

See, people buy anything in the market which is cheap either because they do not know that there is something of a higher quality or they cannot afford it. Why you are driving a beat up Ford is because you either have not driven a BMW or you cannot afford it. You do not know how to get into it.

Once you have driven a BMW you are not going to drive one of those downhill cars. I was driving with somebody in a car recently and he said, "This car goes downhill very well." I said, "That is good!"

Once you have known the pleasure of something of a higher caliber, will you go for something less? No. That is all. I am not against pleasure. I am all for pleasure, but I think it is stupid to go for small pleasures. That is all.

———

"Intensity means... existing here as a piece of life and nothing else... If you just remain a piece of life, your reaching your ultimate nature is a very natural process."

Questioner: What is intensity? What is its role on the spiritual path? How can one be intense all the time?

Sadhguru: How can I tell you what intensity is? Life is intensity. Does the life within slacken even for a moment? What slackens is your mind and your emotion. These are sometimes on, and sometimes off. Do you see how the life within you is constantly breathing? Watch the breath. Does it ever slacken? If it slackens, it means death, isn't it?

When I go on saying, be intense, I am just talking about you becoming like life, not becoming a stupid mind. Right now, you have given too much significance to the thoughts and emotions that happen within you, not to the life that is happening within you. Which is more significant? Is it more significant that you are alive right now or that you are thinking right now?

Your fundamental existence, your aliveness is far more significant than your thoughts and emotions. But please look at your life right now. You never even listen to what your life is saying. You only listen to what your thoughts are saying and what your emotions are saying. Is it not so? If you go by the process of your life – whether you are awake or asleep – it is intense. In sleep, is the life within you slackening? If it slackens, you will not wake up tomorrow morning. No matter what you are doing – whether you are doing something that you like or do not like – your life does not slacken. It is only your mind which says, "Oh, I like this, so I will go with passion after it. This I do not like, so I will not go after it." But your life is not like that. It is always intense.

When I say intense, I do not mean working up a certain level of tension. Intense means to be like life, because you are life. If you think you are a thought, if you think you are an emotion, it means you are all screwed up. You are fundamentally life. If you are constantly aware and think: "I am fundamentally life, nothing else; all the other things are passing things", you will remain intense. There is no other way; life does not know any other way to be. Life is always intense. It is only thought and emotion which deceive you in so many ways, and make you believe many things which are not true.

When you look at the nature of your thoughts or your emotions for that matter, you find that a number of times in your life, they made you believe that "this is it". And after a little while, they made you feel like a fool for what you believed in yesterday. Has it not happened to you? Hasn't this happened with your emotions also? Today your emotions tell you, "This is the most wonderful man", but tomorrow your emotions tell you, "This is the most horrible man." And in both cases it was a hundred percent true. When your emotions told you he was wonderful, it was a hundred percent true. Next day when your emotions told you he was horrible, it was also a hundred percent true.

So your thoughts and emotions are tremendous instruments of deception. They can make you believe anything, just about anything. Please see all the different types of things that people believe. Just look at your own beliefs; none of them will stand any kind of investigation, yes? Most of your beliefs will not withstand three questions. If I ask you three questions, your whole belief system will collapse. But your mind will make you believe different things at different stages in your life, and you firmly believe that they are true.

So intensity means just existing here as a piece of life and nothing else. If you exist here as a piece of life, everything that should happen to this life will naturally happen to you. You do not have to strive and struggle to get somewhere. If you just exist here as life, pure life, life will naturally go to its ultimate nature. You are creating a big distortion and a huge hurdle in the process of life reaching its natural goal, by becoming a thought, by becoming an emotion, by becoming ideas, by becoming opinions, by becoming prejudices, anger, hatred, this and that.

If you just remain a piece of life, your reaching your ultimate nature is a very natural process. It is not something that you have to strive for or struggle for. This is why I have been saying, just maintain your intensity; the rest will happen. You do not have to look for the way to heaven. You just maintain your intensity, and this life goes to its ultimate nature. It will naturally go. Nobody can stop it nor can anybody take it. There is nobody who can take it to its ultimate nature. There is nobody who can stop it from going to its ultimate nature. It is just that we can delay it, inordinately, eternally; or we can just allow it to go very quickly without any obstructions.

So when we say a 'spiritual process', we are trying to allow it to happen as quickly as possible. If this has to happen, you do not have to call for God to come and help you. You just have to become life and life alone and nothing but life.

"Anything in existence, if it travels at the speed of light, it becomes light. Travel at the pace that I move, and you will become me."

Questioner: Sadhguru, this sounds awkward, but I'd like to say it. I want to become like you. Is there such a possibility for me?

Sadhguru: Grow a beard like me. (Laughs) Yesterday somebody asked me a similar question in a different way, and I just reminded them that there is a simple phenomenon in life, in physical existence, that they should be aware of. If you know some physics, you know there that if, for example, you take this piece of metal and throw it at the speed of light, it will not remain a mass as it is now; it will become light. Did you know this?

Anything in existence, if it travels at the speed of light, it becomes light. So everything in existence can be converted into light; if I just move this hand at the speed of light, this hand will no more remain a hand, it will become light. This is a scientific fact.

If you try to plug yourself into an electric socket — like the light bulb — it will do something else to you! You will not become light. So, whatever you consider to be Sadhguru, right now — I do not know what your idea of me is; that is also questionable — if a desire has risen within you, for whatever reason, that you want to become me, then you have to move at the same pace as me.

A very beautiful example was set by Adi Shankara. Adi Shankara was a walking man, you know? He died at the age of thirty-two, but before this he walked up and down this country three times. He even walked the country once or twice sideways, east and west. That is a lot of walking, isn't it? By the time he was thirty-two he did all this walking. But it wasn't the walking that killed him, by the way!

When he walked, his disciples walked behind him. And he set up this device. He demanded that the disciples should walk at his pace. Sometimes he walked very fast, sometimes slow, sometimes at medium speed. Whichever way he walked, everybody was expected to walk at just the same pace. If they walked at the wrong pace, they were reprimanded. He would walk ten miles an hour and everybody had to walk ten miles an hour. He would walk one mile an hour and everybody had to walk one mile an hour. He would walk three miles an hour and everybody had to walk three miles an hour. He would be walking at a certain speed; then he would alter his speed, and everybody had to alter their speed. This was a simple way for him to train his disciples to become him. It was a very physical tool. By simply doing that, he transformed the people who walked behind him.

So if a desire has risen within you that you want to become me, you must start from the end that you know. You cannot start from the end which you do not know. You must have noticed that this morning our meeting started at twelve noon. It is ten pm now; it has been going on continuously for ten hours. Before that we had two or three hours of telephonic meetings. This meeting may continue through the night until tomorrow morning, and I will sit here and go through all that it demands. I will sit here the whole night. I will just be going on with what I have to do, without any irritation, without any agitation; I will just do what I have to do with total involvement.

So start from this end. Learn to conduct the day — no matter what the quality of the day, no matter what kind of people you meet, what kind of situations you face — with the same sense of involvement, with the same dedication to little things and big things. Just do everything with the same sense of involvement and energy, without paying less attention to one thing and more attention to something else. Pay total attention to everything. Start from this end. It can happen. Just do that.

Did you ever see me paying less attention to one person and more attention to another person? Or did you see me pay more attention to one issue than the other? You did not. And whatever the situations have been, or whatever the kind of people, you did not see me get irritated or agitated. Start from that end.

Travel at the speed of light and you will become light. Travel at the pace that I move, and you will become me.

Isha Foundation

Isha Foundation is a non-profit volunteer organization that addresses all aspects of human well-being. From its powerful yoga programs for inner transformation to its inspiring social and environmental projects, Isha activities are designed to create an inclusive culture as a basis for global peace and development. This integral approach has gained worldwide recognition, as reflected in Isha Foundation's Special Consultative Status with the Economic and Social Council (ECOSOC) of the United Nations. Hundreds of thousands of volunteers support the Foundation's work in over 200 centers across the globe.

Sadhguru

A profound mystic and visionary humanitarian, Sadhguru is a spiritual Master with a difference. An arresting blend of profundity and pragmatism, his life and work serve as a reminder that inner sciences are not esoteric disciplines from an outdated past, but vitally relevant to our times.

With speaking engagements that take him around the world, Sadhguru is widely sought after by prestigious global forums such as the United Nations Millennium Peace Summit, the Australian Leadership Retreat and the World Economic Forum.

Isha Yoga

Isha Yoga Programs Isha Yoga offers a unique possibility for individuals to empower themselves and reach their full potential. Designed by Sadhguru to suit individuals from every social and cultural background, Isha Yoga programs extend a rare opportunity for self-discovery and inner transformation under the guidance of an enlightened Master.

Isha Yoga Center

Isha Yoga Center, founded under the aegis of Isha Foundation, is located at the Velliangiri Foothills amidst a forest reserve with abundant wildlife. Created as a powerful center for inner growth, this popular destination attracts people from all parts of the world.

Dhyanalinga Yogic Temple

The Dhyanalinga is a powerful and unique energy form – the essence distilled of yogic sciences. The Dhyanalinga Yogic Temple is a meditative space that does not ascribe to any particular faith or belief system nor requires any ritual, prayer or worship. The vibrational energies of the Dhyanalinga allow even those unaware of meditation to experience a deep state of meditativeness, revealing the essential nature of life.

Isha Rejuvenation

Isha Rejuvenation offers unique, carefully scientifically structured programs designed by Sadhguru to bring vibrancy and optimal balance to one's life energies, thus facilitating healthy living as well as the prevention and uprooting of chronic ailments.

Isha Outreach

One life, touching another...

Action for Rural Rejuvenation

A longtime vision of Sadhguru, Action for Rural Rejuvenation (ARR) is a unique, well defined philanthropic effort to restore and raise the human spirit and rejuvenate the marginalized rural population – physically, mentally, socially and spiritually. ARR is implementing models of community-based, sustainable development while reviving the indigenous culture and knowledge and also offers free primary and preventive healthcare.

Project GreenHands

Project GreenHands (PGH) is an ecological initiative of Isha Foundation to prevent and reverse environmental degradation and enable sustainable living. The Project aims to plant 114 million trees all across Tamil Nadu – providing an additional 10% to the existing tree coverage in the state. Project GreenHands has been awarded the prestigious *Indira Gandhi Paryavaran Puraskar* (IGPP) by the Indian Ministry of Environment and Forests for its significant contributions in the fields of environmental protection, conservation, regeneration and awareness creation.

Isha Vidhya – An Isha Education Initiative

Isha Vidhya offers education as a life-empowering opportunity for rural children. Affordable to even the most economically disadvantaged families, Isha Vidhya is opening a new door for rural children to pursue a better future. Over the coming years, Isha Vidhya will set up 206 schools, one for each of Tamil Nadu's taluks (counties), changing the educational landscape of rural India.

Isha Home School

Isha Home School, set in the tranquil surroundings of the Velliangiri Foothills, offers a stimulating environment for the inner blossoming of each child. Isha Home School helps each student reach his or her true potential and enhances his or her natural and latent talents while maintaining high standards of academic excellence.

Isha Craft & Isha Raiment

Isha Craft and Isha Raiment bring a touch of Isha into people's lives through gift items, jute pieces, paintings, metal crafts, stone art-de-facts and handicrafts, as well as designer clothing which includes casual, formal and yoga wear. All profits from these ventures are used to serve the rural people of India through Action for Rural Rejuvenation (ARR).

Isha Publications

Isha Publications is dedicated to offering Sadhguru's candid and thought-provoking works and discourses in the form of books and booklets, CDs and DVDs. Other Isha releases include music by *Sounds of Isha* and other artists, special event footage, Isha's monthly magazine *Forest Flower* and the Tamil magazine *Kaattu Poo*.

CONTACT US:

INDIA
Isha Yoga Center
Velliangiri Foothills
Semmedu (P.O.)
Coimbatore-641 114, India
Tel. +91-422-2515345
IYC@ishafoundation.org

USA
Isha Institute of InnerSciences
951, Isha Lane
McMinnville, TN-37110, USA
Tel: +1-931-668-1900
usa@ishafoundation.org

UNITED KINGDOM
Isha Institute of Inner Sciences
P.O. Box 559
Isleworth, TW7 5WR, UK
Tel: +44-7956998729
uk@ishafoundation.org

For more information on your local Isha Center, please visit our website:www.ishafoundation.org